KISWAHILI: PAST, PRESENT AND FUTURE HORIZONS

KISWAHILI: PAST, PRESENT AND FUTURE HORIZONS

Rocha Chimerah

Nairobi University Press

First published 1998 by
Nairobi University Press
University of Nairobi
P.O. Box 30197
Nairobi

Reprinted with minor revision 2000

ISBN: 9-9668463-52

© Rocha M. Chimerah

Front Cover Photograph: Longonot (telecommunication)
earth station, Kenya Courtesy of International
and Public Relations Department, Telkom Kenya Limited.

University of Nairobi Library CIP Data
   Chimera, Rocha
   Kiswahili: past present and future / R. Chimera. - Nairobi:
   Nairobi University Press, 1998.
   152 pp.
   1. Swahili language. I Title

PL 8701 .C54

ISBN 9966 846 35 2

Printed by Sunlitho Ltd., P.O. Box 13939, Nairobi, Kenya.

Contents

	Page
Preface	ix

PART 1 KISWAHILI: AN AFRICAN ALTERNATIVE TO IMPORTED EUROPEAN LANGUAGE?

CHAPTER 1: Kiswahili's Incredible Triumph 1
The Lingua-Franca 1
Mother-Tongue and Second Language 2
National and Official Language 3
Language of Instruction in East and Central Africa 3
As a Subject Elsewhere 4
Archives 6
Institutes of Kiswahili Research 6
Radio Stations 7
Recent Advances in Kiswahili 7

CHAPTER 2: An African Alternative to Imported European Languages 19

CHAPTER 3: Kiswahili: A Language Steeped in Controversy 25
The Arab-Descent Theory 25
Concerning Semitic Claims 28
Pidginisation Claims 28
The Hybrid and Impoverished-Vocabulary Theories 29
Comparison with English 31
The Epitome of Hybridisation 32
Borrowing as Strength 33
Borrowing in Kiswahili 35
The "Jungu Kuu" Camp 36
The "Wanamapinduzi" or Revolutionaries Camp 40
The "Anglophile" Camp 41
The English Way 42
Of a Journal, Writers and New Coinages 44

CHAPTER 4: English as the Language of Instruction in Kenya 47
Background 47
The English Language Question Globally 57
India 59
Britain 60
West Africa 62
Singapore 63
Malaysia 63
The Language of Instruction 64
But Why Not All in ... Kiswahili? 66

PART II: KISWAHILI: THE RISE AND TRIUMPH OF AN INTERNATIONAL LANGUAGE

CHAPTER 5: Status of Kiswahili in East and Central Africa Within a Continental Context 73
Background 73
Trade 74
Religion 75
Politics 76

CHAPTER 6: The Spread of Kiswahili in Eastern and Central Africa 79
Tanzania 79
Kenya 87
Uganda 111
The Democratic Republic of Congo 121

CHAPTER 7: Kiswahili in the Rest of Africa 127
Africa: The Tower of Babel 127
Why not Another African Language? 129
The Nigerians 130
The Zimbabwean 131
Soyinka's Word 132
The Organisation of African Unity 132

INDEX 137

Preface

The articles in this book were written in 1989. Two of them, namely "Lingua Franca" and "In Praise" were entered for the first African Languages and Linguistics Conference held in Nairobi in July 1991.

Ever since 1989, Kiswahili has made a lot of strides in many areas. For instance, the language has gained a lot of novel lexical items over those years. This has made it cope with fast-changing global requirements. Most of the new words in Kiswahili have been borrowed from languages whose native speakers are leading in the all-cencompassing modern day information technology. However, quite a good percentage of words entering Kiswahili today are coinages by Swahili scholars and artists. There is also a significant percentage of vocabulary items from other African languages within the Swahili speaking region which have forced their way into Kiswahili proper. In Kenya for example, some Kikuyu words such as *irio* and *githeri* are known to, and used by, every speaker of Kiswahili when speaking this language.

Coinages by Kiswahili scholars and writers include such words as *ukimwi* (AIDS), *upili* (secondary), *runinga* (television) *zutafindaki/ndaki* (University/varsity), *tarakilishi* (computer), *mangala* (microscope), *uka* (ray), *ukamramba* (X-ray) and *ningala* (telescope) among many others. It should be noted that a lot of the new coinages are labels of electronics and other items in the domain of science. In this regard, it is quite clear that Kiswahili is not, in any way, being left behind in this dynamic, sophisticated area.

Which brings us to the language's greatest stride so far; namely, its place in cyber technology. Kiswahili has been one lucky African language that has always attracted enthusiasts from outside the continent. This has helped the language tremendously since the West has been leading in modern-day developments ever since the industrial revolution in Britain and later the United States of America. The whole process (of Kiswahili's runaway development) started with missionaries, mainly British, standardising the Zanzibar dialect, Kiunguja in the first half of this century. This standardised dialect has, ever since, become the mainstream Kiswahili, eclipsing even the more prestigious and arguably more sophisticated dialects of the northern Swahililand, such as Kimvita (the dialect of Mombasa in Kenya) and Kiamu (the dialect of Lamu and neighbouring islands in northern Kenya coast).

The second major step for Kiswahili was the taming of its grammar. This major step was taken firstly by Elizabeth Ashton (a Briton) and then by Edgar Polome (an American). These have recently been updated by Ireri Mbaabu (a Kenyan) who is the first person to write Kiswahili grammar in the language.

However, the greatest step, so far, is finding a place for Kiswahili in cyber-space technology. It has been predicted that in the 21st century, those languages that will not have their own computer vocabulary will be left behind and eventually die off. Fortunately for Kiswahili, it has many enthusiasts in the one country that leads in this type of technology: the USA. That more than 100 universities in the USA offer Kiswahili as a taught subject is a big boost for the language. Some of the most prestigious universities in that country, including Harvard, Yale, Cornell and UCLA, are at the forefront in offering the language as a subject of study, something that has the potential of really boosting the status of Kiswahili in that country and the world-over in the 21st century. There was a time when Kiswahili was taught only by Africans, mostly from East Africa, in these universities but these days, the language is taught by Americans themselves who are as good as the East African instructors of English are to their own Anglophone pupils. It is in this context that we must view cyber-space Kiswahili, and that is what this book is all about.

The Kiswahili enthusiasts from the USA in particular have now completed compiling its potential computer vocabulary. In this context, Kiswahili's computer language is a reality.

The center of these activities is Yale University where professor Anne Bierstekker, a renowned Kiswahili scholar who taught at Kenyatta College in the late 60s, leads the pack in ensuring the success of Kiswahili. Assisted by Kenyan and Tanzanian scholars resident in the USA such as professor Al-Amin Mazrui (Ohio State University) and Professor Ebrahim Noor Sharrif (Rutgers University, New Jersey), Professor Bierstekker's project is poised to be the greatest single achievement as far as this African language is concerned. In this regard, Kiswahili is doubtlessly going places, come the 21st century.

Finally I wish to state that it is high time Africans did their own things themselves, for themselves and the rest of humanity. It is encouraging that the East African Cooperation has been revived. This revival is good news because it is bound to give Kiswahili a second chance to spread and cover the whole of the region. The news get better if one takes into consideration that Rwanda, a country whose nationals speak Kiswahili as well as Kenyans do, has also applied to join the Cooperation. And after Burundi solves her political crisis, it is expected that she will also join the others in the region, thus making it easy for more Swahili-speaking peoples to communicate in the language. In addition to the above developments, it is not too early to predict that the Democratic Republic of Congo is poised to be a significant fertile ground for Kiswahili's consolidation of speakers westwards, thanks to President Laurent D. Kabila's preference for languages of the masses.

Given this scenario, the leadership in these countries will do their people a great service if they set aside funds for the language's further development. This is a challenge those in leadership have to face especially since it is policies of the German colonialists, for one, that were responsible for the enviable spread of Kiswahili in Tanzania and Rwanda/Burundi, and not our own. It should also be remembered that it is under the British colonialists that Kiswahili was standardised. Surely, if the much hated colonialists could take the initial, very crucial stages in developing and helping to spread our language, shouldn't we feel more bound to do even better? Are we willing to do anything for our own language, or should we continue despising it while, at the same time, continue adoring English, French and Portuguese? Are we doomed to be dominated for ever culturally by way of languages? I say no! We should do something about this now .

ROCHA M. CHIMERAH
Egerton University
January 1998

KISWAHILI:
AN AFRICAN ALTERNATIVE TO IMPORTED EUROPEAN LANGUAGES?

PART 1

Chapter One

Kiswahili's Incredible Triumph

The Lingua-Franca

Kiswahili can claim to be the East and Central African region's foremost language of wider communication. This is the case even in the face of a very rich and varied multiplicity of languages across this vast area and the relentless rivalry from the two topmost, powerful European languages, namely English and French. Against all odds, Kiswahili has made tremendous strides over the period between the first half of the 18th Century and this Century. The result of its impressive expansion as an inter-ethnic lingua franca is that it has reached its present eminence as the most widely spoken language in Africa trans-nationally, with the probable exception of Arabic, which claims several countries in the Nothern part of the continent.

Other notable trans-ethnic lingua francas in Africa are Hausa, Bambara and Wolof, all in West Africa. In terms of merit, however, and especially in the context of a continent that has earned itself the rather unenviable label of "Tower of Babel" due to the great diversity of its socio-politico-linguistic groups, these other lingua francas, together with Arabic, lack Kiswahili's critical appeal as a politically neutral language. It is the only language in Africa that is free from any association with an ethnicity-conscious "tribe": The original native speakers of the language, the Waswahili of Kenyan, Tanzanian and Mozambican coasts are, on the whole, an extremely detribalised polity the continent-over if not the world-over.

Mother-Tongue and Second Language

Kiswahili's main locality is East and Central Africa. It is spoken as a mother-tongue by its original "tribes", collectively known as the Waswahili, of the coastal littoral of Kenya and Tanzania (including the islands of Zanzibar and Pemba) and embracing coastal territory as far South as Mozambique and the northern tip of Madagascar (known by the Waswahili as Bukini). People other than the Waswahili who speak it as a mother tongue are Swahilised Arabs, some of whom have had it as their mother tongue for several centuries spanning from around the 12th Century to date. Other Swahilised peoples are found in the Democratic Republic of Congo, Zaire, Malawi, Mozambique, Southern Somalia and the Comoros. Then there are the Swahili-speaking Northern Madagascans in Bukini, who also speak it as a mother-tongue (Polome, 1967; Whiteley, 1969; Salim, 1974).

The majority of Swahili speakers, however, speak it as mother tongue as well as a second language. This is so in areas like Tanzania, the rest of Kenya, Northern Uganda and also some pockets in the Luganda-dominated South, East and North-Eastern Congo, Rwanda, Burundi, Northern Zambia (bordering Tanzania and Zaire), Northern Malawi and the Lake region, Southern Somalia, Northern Mozambique (bordering Tanzania) and Northern Madagascar (Prins, 1961; Polome, 1967; Whiteley, 1969). Kiswahili is also spoken as a mother-tongue as well as a second language in the Island of Sokotra, off the Horn of Africa (Whiteley, 1969).

A recent development is that the language is spoken by about a third of Oman's total population as a mother-tongue. Kiswahili speakers in Oman are Arab-descended migrants from East Africa, the greatest majority coming from the islands of Zanzibar and Pemba, who retraced the steps of their distant forefathers to reclaim their ancentry in that oil-rich modern nation.

National and Official Language

Kiswahili is the national language of both Kenya and Tanzania. While the official language in Kenya is still English, in Tanzania Kiswahili has this status to its credit as well. The language thus permeates all spheres of life in Tanzania whereas in Kenya it shares the political mantle with English but dominates social interaction as well as urban life at a non-official pedestal. Nevertheless, in both countries, it is viewed as the language of national unity particularly against the backdrop of a multiplicity of ethnic groupings with a myriad of languages within each country's borders; Tanzania leading Kenya by at least 3 to 1 in this respect.

Language of Instruction in East and Central Africa

Kiswahili is the language of instruction at the Primary school level of the educational system in Tanzania. At the secondary school and university levels, English wields more influence. In Kenya, Kiswahili tends to be the language of instruction in the first three grades of primary school in areas where it is the mother-tongue, and also in urban areas where people are relatively detribalised. It is also the language of instruction in areas bordering the coastal region, where there is lack of written materials in various mother-tongues. In all other areas, the different mother-tongues are the languages of instruction in the first three grades. From the fourth grade onwards, English takes over from all indigenous Kenyan languages as the language of instruction.

The situation seems to be similar in the Comoros where French takes over from Comorian Kiswahili (the dialects Kingazija, Kinzwani and Kiunguja) as the language of instruction (Whiteley, 1969). In Congo, French supplanted Kiswahili as the language of instruction at all levels of the school system in the areas where the latter has a majority of speakers. At present, Kiswahili is used as the primary school instructional medium only in the deep rural areas in Shaba Province (formerly Katanga), East and Northeastern Congo (Whiteley, 1969).

Kiswahili is taught as an examinable subject in Kenya and Tanzania at the primary and secondary school levels. In the other Kiswahili-speaking countries mentioned above, the language is most probably taught as a subject although it may not exactly be in a position to receive the attention that it enjoys in the countries where it reflects unity at the national level.

As a Subject Elsewhere

Kiswahili is offered as a foreign language subject in approximately 100 universities across the United States of America. Significantly, it is among the foreign languages offered as a subject of study at all the prestigious universities in the U.S.A. such as Havard, Yale, Cornell, U.C.L.A. etc. Other Universities are Ohio State at Columbus, Ohio at Athens Ohio, University of Illinois Urbana-Champaigne, Northern Illinois University at DeKalb, Michigan State University, Florida at Gainsville, St. Lawrence, Stanford, Berkeley, North Western, Syracuse, N.Y., Texas at Austin and Wisconsin at Madison, to mention just a few.

In Britain, the University of London and York University offer Kiswahili to both home and overseas students. London and Cambridge universities have a long history of interest in Kiswahili and have for years been offering examinations at the G.C.E. certificate to overseas students at both the 'O' and 'A' levels.

Other countries whose universities offer Kiswahili as a foreign language include Germany, South Korea, Ghana and Japan. The list may not be exhaustive but the information offered here is what was available to the author. These universities conduct annual in-country programmes of intensive study of Kiswahili in East Africa.

Furthermore, quite a number of countries have been sending their students out to the Kiswahili-speaking countries - notably Kenya and Tanzania for intensive study of the language. Participants in these programmes have always been university students.

So far the U.S. programme is the most elaborate of them all. Being a federal government-sponsored programme, it involves students who have studied the language in their various colleges for at least two years and can handle it from tolerably well to very well. Their coming to East Africa, therefore, is to polish what they already know.

Also involved are American professors who have made a name in the U.S. linguistic circles and who, their linguistics achievement apart, speak Kiswahili fluently or at least tolerably well. Those who have participated, so far, are professors Ivan Dihoff (Yale, then Ohio State), Ann Bierstekker (Northern Illinois, DeKalb, then Yale), Heinnebusch (U.C.L.A.), Eyamba Bokamba (University of Illinois at Urbana-Champaigne). Two Ph.D. candidates have also been involved as assistant directors. The programme is trying to filter into Masters and Ph.D. curriculae.

Africa has been instrumental in providing instructors. In Kenya, for example, those involved are well known personalities in linguistics and Kiswahili from the crop of Swahili lecturers at both Nairobi and Kenyatta Universities. Professor Mohammed Abdulaziz of Nairobi University for instance has been the Kenyan director and coordinator of the programme while Professors Ireri Mbaabu and Chacha Nyaigotti Chacha, have been the Kenyan assistant directors and coordinators at different times. On the other hand, a very well-known Kiswahili scholar, Ahmed Sheikh Nabhany, has been the programme's cultural coordinator. Others are the late Ezekiel Kadenge Kazungu, the late Professor Jay Kitsao, Mohammed Bakari, Rocha Chimerah and Dr. Kimani Njogu.

Archives

Kiswahili promoters in East Africa widely believe that a lot of 16th to 19th Century Kiswahili literature is buried in German and British university archives. Some self-appointed witnesses have come to reveal that some of the oldest Kiswahili texts, written in the original Arabic as well as Latin scripts, are in American universities such as U.C.L.A. and Stanford, neatly stacked in guarded sections of their libraries. One may also find old Kiswahili stories, collected and published by European Kiswahili enthusiasts such as Bishop Steere, adorning the shelves of universities that have a relatively shorter tradition with Kiswahili like Ohio University, Athens. Such invaluable, long-history manuscripts and texts are not found in the libraries of East Africa from where they originated. Neither can they be found in the national archives in this region.

Institutes of Kiswahili Research

Currently, there are three institutes involved in Kiswahili research in East Africa. Two are in Tanzania, the *Taasisi* in Zanzibar, and the Institute of Kiswahili Research at the University of Dar-es-Salaam. Kenya recently established her own Institute of Kiswahili research at the University of Nairobi although it has not made much progress.

All these institutes deal primarily with the development of Kiswahili language. Kiswahili literature, nevertheless, is one of their concerns. The institutes coordinate with experts within and outside the universities to bring to the fore any materials and/or findings that are worthwhile for the language's development. Renowned research fellows are attached to the institutes.

Radio Stations

In Africa, Kenya, Tanzania, Zanzibar, Rwanda, Burundi, Uganda and South Africa have Kiswahili services on their national radio stations. People in Africa thus can tune to Kiswahili programmes on Kenya Broadcasting Corporation (KBC) Nairobi, Radio Tanzania, Dar-es-Salaam and Zanzibar, Radio Rwanda, Kigali, Voice of Uganda, Kampala, Radio South Africa (R.S.A.) Johannesburg, Channel Africa, Johannesburg, and listen to their favourite programmes in their world-renowned lingua franca.

Outside Africa, there are the Kiswahili services of the British Broadcasting Corporation BBC, *Sauti ya Ujerumani*, Cologne (Radio Deutsche Welle), Radio Moscow, *Idhaa ya Kiswahili*, Beijing, China, (Kiswahili Service), Voice of America, U.S.A., India, etc. The list of radio stations mentioned here may not be exhaustive. It is perhaps in this context that Chinua Achebe commented that almost every major radio station in the world today broadcasts services in Kiswahili thus giving the impression that this language is a mega-tongue in Africa, whereas he (Achebe) did not think it was. We may need to give him the benefit of a doubt as he may probably have changed his mind in regard to his perception of the language since a lot of researchers and political movements have ever since revealed its (Kiswahili's) authenticity and centrality in African affairs.

Recent Advances in Kiswahili

(I) The dictionaries

After almost two decades of anticipation, East and Central Africa can grace their shelves, libraries and schools with the most up-to-date Kiswahili-Kiswahili dictionary - a work that was long overdue. The dictionary was the brain-child of the Institute of Kiswahili Research, University of Dar-es-Salaam, and it embraced talents from a cross-section of the Kiswahili-speaking region. Those involved in the research and completion of the work were:-

- Professor George Mhina from Tanga, Tanzania - a professor of language and linguistics, University of Dar-es-Salaam.
- Hamisi Akida, from Tanga, Tanzania - a senior research fellow at the University of Dar-es-Salaam.
- Yohanna Mganga from Tanga, Tanzania - a senior research fellow.
- Sheikh Mohamed Ali of Tanga, Tanzania.
- M. Burhan Mkelle, from Zanzibar, Tanzania - a research fellow.
- Muhsin Alidina from Zanzibar, Tanzania - a research fellow.
- Jaafar Tejani from Zanzibar, Tanzania - a university lecturer.
- Abdilatif Abdallah from Mombasa, Kenya - a senior research fellow, University of Dar-es-Salaam (now the editor of *Africa Events*, London).
- Tigiti Sengo from Dar-es-Salaam, Tanzania - an assistant research fellow.
- Ms. Zubeida Tumbo from Dar-es-Salaam, Tanzania - an assistant research fellow.
- Joseph Kiimbila from Bukoba, Tanzania.
- Canute W. Temu from Moshi, Tanzania - an assistant research fellow.
- David Massamba from Musoma, Tanzania - a research fellow and professor.
- Prof. Rajmund Ohly from Polland.

(Mhina, et al. 1981, p.v.), to mention but a few.

The dictionary stands as an impressive piece of work to date "with a total of not less than 50,000 vocabulary items" (Mhina, et al. 1981, blurb), apart from other features like proverbs and idioms which abound in it.

Apart from this work, there is also the dictionary of medical terms due to be published in Kenya. Panelists for this work, during its formulation phase, were led by Professor Mohammed Abdulaziz of the University of Nairobi. Like its predecessor, this work involved Kiswahili scholars from Kenya and Tanzania. Among them were Professor Mkude of the University of Dar-es-Salaam, and the energetic self-made Kiswahili scholar mentioned earlier, Ahmad Sheikh Nabhany of Mombasa, Kenya. When this dictionary is finally published, it will go a long way to supplement the other dictionaries already in the field including the one mentioned above, and the dictionary of science and technology terminology.

Prior to these works, the field was littered with flimsy dictionaries that made Kiswahili look like it did not have enough vocabulary to communicate anything serious. Almost all of them had been put together by individuals whose over-riding concern for the development of Kiswahili must be appreciated. Such individuals are like the late Frederick Johnson whose immortal pioneering works, *Swahili-English* and *English-Kiswahili* dictionaries, together with the *Swahili-Swahili* dictionary *Kamusi ya Kiswahili*, dominated the scene for decades and served the entire Kiswahili scholarship admirably. Other works were: *Simplified Swahili* by P.M. Wilson, Ludwig Krapf's and Edward Steere's dictionaries, grammar books such as *Teach Yourself Swahili*, and several bilingual Swahili-French, Swahili-German as well as Italian-Swahili dictionaries authored primarily for tourists' use.

(ii) Old wine in new bottles

Of recent, the same Ahmad Sheikh Nabhany has become a leading advocate for a going-back-to-the-roots approach to Kiswahili's lexical enrichment. The basis of this approach is simply to use original Kiswahili/Kingozi words in place of the Arabic words which are in currency in modern Kiswahili or, otherwise, to use them as complements to the Arabic derivations, or as synonyms. For example, Nabhany is in favour of the use of words such as *mbawazi* (sympathy/empathy), *mkata* (poor person), *mbeko* (respect[noun]), *tungo* (poem), *liwaa* (forget), *choyo* (selfishness), *mkwasi* (rich person) *mavuyo/bwerere* (cheap, easy), *zeo/mwiya* (time) etc., instead of their Arabic-derived equivalents currently in popular usage; that is: *huruma, maskini, heshima, shairi, sahau, bakhili, tajiri, rahisi* and *wakati* respectively.

Nabhany has compiled a list of these vocabularies. His hypothesis is that there is an original Kiswahili word for every Arabic loan word. Whether this idea is foolproof or not has yet to go through the test of research. What is of great consequence now is whether more original Kiswahili words can be unearthed with the aid of committed research. If this can be done, the language may gain a great deal to boost the quite impressive 50,000-plus total vocabulary count (TVC) already in day-to-day currency. This count compares quite well with a good number of metropolitan languages, some of the most well-known among them, like French, having only twice as much, against a long tradition of exhaustive research and meticulously planned development. It should be borne in mind that the full potential, capacity, and worth of Kiswahili has hardly been scratched, taking into account that the amount of research on and within the language so far conducted, is meagre compared to other international languages.

(iii) *Translated or interpreted foreign concepts*

Another approach to language development as advocated by Ahmad Sheikh Nabhany, among others, is to directly translate or interpret novel concepts from a given donor language (DL) to the target language (TL), i.e. the local language. The Arabs have used this method for centuries to develop their language and are still using it to this day. All indications point to the fact that it has served them well, Arabic being one of the languages topping the list of famous global tongues.

Through this approach, Nabhany brought into modern Kiswahili words like *uka* (ray), *zuka/nyuka* (rays), *uka-mraba* (X-ray) and *mangala* (microscope) among others. Following his footsteps, one may find it not only easy but also very interesting to think of words such as *chakucha/chakuamsha* (breakfast) *chakushindia/chakushindisha* (lunch), *chakuchwia/chakuchwisha* (dinner) and *chakulaza* (supper). For computer, the words *tarakili* or *tarakilishine/tarakilishi* are suggested, *tarakilishi* actually being preferred.

These words have been formed by both interpreting the English concepts (which have no strict equivalents in Kiswahili) and combining two or more Kiswahili concepts that answer to the denotation. To wit, *chakucha* is a combination of *chakula* (food) and *kucha* (dawn); in full, *chakula cha kucha* (which may be English-translated as "dawn food"). The third syllable of the word *chakula* is dropped and then *cha* which is the root morpheme of the word *kucha* which combines the infinitive *ku* (to) and *cha* (dawn), is added to *chaku*. The result is the emergence of the hitherto non-existent word *chakucha*. The same approach has been applied in forming the words *chakushindia* (*chakula* + *shindia*, the latter word-segment meaning "pass the day with"). Similarly, *chakuchwia* simply combines *chakula*, with *la* dropped, and *chwia* (pass the evening with). *Chakulaza* has been created in the same manner with *chaku(la)* and *laza* (which means send to bed) being the two original words that have been merged to make the new compound word.

The process of creating *tarakili* and *tarakilishine/ tarakilishi*, is the same as above. Interpreted, these words mean "brain that computes"*(tarakili)*; machine that computes like a brain" (*tarakilishine/tarakilishi*).

Tarakili has been formed by combining *tarakimu* (with the last two syllables dropped) and *akili* (with the first syllable dropped). The two words, *tarakimu* and *akili* mean numbers or figures and brain respectively; and they are both Swahilised from Arabic. *Tarabongo* may be used in place of *tarakili* to mean the same and replacing the Arabic loan word *akili* with *ubongo*, the original Kiswahili word for brain, dropping the initial syllable *u* in the process, and at the same time adhering to Nabhany's approach of replacing loans with Bantu-Kiswahili words. *Tarakilishine* on the other hand is formed by combining *tarakimu* (with *kimu* dropped) and *akili* (with initial *a* dropped) and *mashine* (with initial syllable, *ma*, dropped) a swahilised word from the English term *machine* (in Kiswahili, the final letter is pronounced). The new word *tarakilishine* means a machine that computes like a brain. The other word, *tarakilishi* is closely related to *tarakilishine* and its interpretation is exactly the same. The only difference between these words is that the final syllable of the word *tarakilishine* has been dropped thus leaving behind the word *tarakilishi* which is less mouthful and perfectly fits Kiswahili phonology as well as morphology.

It would not be surprising if this word adheres to the behavioural patterns of other parts of speech in Kiswahili such as the verb, so that words like *tarakilisha* (compute), *kutarakilisha* (to compute) and *nitarakilishie* (compute for me) gain common currency.

Chakuamsha (food that wakes a person up), *chakushindisha* (food that helps a person pass the day) and *chakuchwisha* (food that helps a person pass the evening) are hereby suggested as either alternatives, equivalents or synonyms of *chakucha*, *chakushindia* and *chakuchwia* respectively. The recommendation here is that the first and second sets of words be used as synonyms.

It is necessary to underline that this approach has hitherto been employed in English language as has been done here. This is how the American word *brunch* (breakfast: b̲r̲ + lunch: unch), now in popular usage possibly throughout the English-speaking world, was created. Back in Kenya, the word *Ukimwi* (AIDS) from *Ukosefu wa Kinga Mwilini* (lack of immunity in the body) was created in the same manner by the *Lugha Yetu* Radio Group.

At this juncture, it will be observed that once this approach is accepted as a legitimate method of creating words in all of the Kiswahili-speaking areas, Kiswahili scholars and enthusiasts will wake up to the realisation that their subsequent dictionaries may be considerably beefed up in this manner. As a matter of consequence, their language will have gotten an all-time monumental boost. This is more so as swahilised English words such as *lunch* (Kiswahili: *lanchi*) and computer (Kiswahili: *kompyuta*) are already in everyday usage. The translated or interpreted concepts will, hence, be synonyms of the swahilised items where they already exist, thereby enriching the language even further.

(iv) Quality radio programmes

Recently, the Kenya Broadcasting Corporation radio service (the national radio station in Nairobi) introduced quite a number of quality radio programmes that have turned out to be a tremendous boon in the light of the country's meagre resources. Arguably, such programmes as *Lugha Yetu* and *Ukumbi wa Kiswahili* have effectively shed the notion of the radio as just an entertainment machine. Both programmes handle Kiswahili academic stuff of high calibre. Since all the participating personalities in both the programmes are either university lecturers or renowned Kiswahili poets and/or self-made scholars, they produce a very erudite programme, educationally. More often than not, they discuss what is offered as curricula content at both university and high school levels.

The same may be said of the national television programme *Sanaa ya Kiswahili*. The chairman of the programme is currently a high school Kiswahili scholar. He invites high school pupils from all over the country to participate in debates, literary criticism of selected examination texts, Kiswahili grammar, oral literature in Kiswahili and recitation and analysis of poetry - all in Kiswahili.

This programme has not only revealed the success and quality of Kiswahili television programmes of its nature in Kenya, but has furthermore most significantly shown that Kiswahili truly deserves its status as Kenya's national language. For, in spite of the completely varied backgrounds of the participating children, some of whom come from regions whose original inhabitants were thought to be impervious to Kiswahili, the Kiswahili they use in *Sanaa ya Kiswahili* is very very impressive. All the participants exude confidence in manipulating their national language on T.V.

(v) Research on new forms of Kiswahili

In Nairobi, a new form of Kiswahili has surfaced and it seems poised to conquer the entire population of the city's youths. This language is pidgin Kiswahili popularly known by its users as "sheng" (probably Swahili + English: Sh + Eng).

Sheng has Kiswahili's grammatical structure although its vocabulary consists of almost equal numbers of Kiswahili and English words with the former having a slight edge over the latter. The rest of its Total Vocabulary Count (TVC) consists of items from other Kenyan languages, notably Gikuyu, Luo, Kamba, Luhya, Hindi/Gujerati, Arabic to mention but a few. Most of the words in the original languages are distorted in pronunciation so that their origins are difficult to pin down. On the other hand, the contexts in which words are used in sheng may be very removed from their original contexts in the original languages. This also may lead to a comprehension block for non-sheng users.

Words like *ngolo* (from English *girl* in distorted Gikuyu pronunciation) will be unrecognisable to both the traditional Gikuyu speaker and the standard English speaker. It will also be incomprehensible to the sophisticated urban Kiswahili speaker. Examples abound: a sheng speaker says *brand* in a Kiswahili sentence to mean *new*. So when he or she says: "Ile *motii* ni *brand*", the hearer should understand the speaker to mean: "that motorcar is brand new (in Kiswahili, motorcar is *motokaa*; a swahilisation of the English word).

Here is a list of some sheng vocabulary:

Ashara	"10-shilling note" (from Arabic/Kiswahili, meaning ten).
Bango	"one-shilling coin" (old usage. From colloquial Kiswahili).
Chuani	"50-cent piece" (from Kiswahili *thumni/sumni*).
Dala	"one shilling coin" (from American English *dollar*).
Fathee/Buda	"father" (from English: father, and Hindi/Gujerati budha).
Goto	"10- cent piece" (old usage. From Kiswahili, meaning knuckle originally).
Hebu kem?	"could you please come?" (Kiswahili and English).
Ingo/dallas	'home" (from Luhya/Luo).
Ingokho	"chicken" (from Luhya).
Karao	"policeman" (from Kiswahili *karai*: the metal cap riot policemen wear looks like this toilet vessel).
Katoyi	"little child" (from Kiswahili *kitoto*, meaning the same).
Kem	"come" (from English come).
Kobole	"5-shilling coin" (origin unknown).
Kunyweta	"to drink" (from Kiswahili *kunywa*; to drink).
Madhee	"mother" (from English: *mother*).

Mob	"a lot: quantity" (from English *mob*. In sheng it changes meaning).
Msosi	"food" (probably from English *sause* with a Kiswahili Class 3 noun marker).
Msosi mob	"a lot of food".
Mtoyi	"child" (from Kiswahili *mtoto*, meaning the same).
Mundu khu mundu	"man to man" (from Luhya).
Ng'oti	"10-cent piece" (from Dholuo *tongolo*, meaning the same).
Oruch	"5-cent piece" (from Kiswahili *ndururu*, meaning the same).
Pao	"pound" (twenty-shilling note, from English *pound*).
Shosho/grams	"grandmother" (from Gikuyu/American English).
Soket /"soo"	"100 - shilling note" (from English socket).
So	"100-shilling note" (short for *soket* in sheng).
Uchi	"go" (origin unkown).
Ushagoo	"rural home" (from Gikuyu gicagi).

Sheng has thus evolved to be almost a full-blown "language". As such, it has necessitated research to determine its origin, usage and development. This is forthcoming in the unpublished work of Al-Amin Mazrui, a professor at Ohio State University in the U.S.A., formerly a lecturer at Kenyatta University, Nairobi.

References

Achebe, Chinua (1975). *Morning Yet on Creation Day*, Heinnemann, London.

Mhina, George, et al. (1981). *Kamusi ya Kiswahili Sanifu* Oxford University Press and Institute of Kiswahili Research, University of Dar-es-Salaam, Dar-es-Salaam.

Nabhany, Ahmed Sheikh (1987). "*Aswili ya Waswahili*", unpublished article, Mombasa, Kenya.

Polome, Edgar (1967). *Swahili Language Handbook*, Centre for Applied Linguistics, Washington D.C.

Prins, A.H.J. (1961). *The Swahili-Speaking Peoples of Zanzibar and the East African Coast*, London.

Salim, Ahmed Idha (1974). "Native or non-Native? The Problem of Identity and the Social Stratification of the Arab-Swahili of Kenya". In B.A. Ogot (ed.) *Hadith 6*, East African Literature Bureau, Nairobi.

Whiteley, Wilfred H. (1969). *Swahili: The Rise of a National Language*, Methuen and Co., London.

Chapter Two

An African Alternative to Imported European Languages

The early history of the long drawn-out struggle between the colonial languages (English, French, Portuguese and to a lesser extent, and for a limited period, German) on one hand and indigenous African languages on the other, has been discussed with a good measure of thoroughness by Whiteley (1969). Whiteley recounted the struggle in the mid-19th Century between two missionary groups, the Mombasa-based Church Missionary Society (C.M.S.) under the Rev. Dr. Ludwig Krapf, and the Zanzibar-based United Mission to Central Africa (UMCA) under the Rev. Dr. Steere, to standardise Kiswahili.

The bitter contest between Kiswahili and English in East Africa has been recounted over and over again by distinguished religious leaders, scholars, politicians, government sponsored educational commissioners, linguists, UNESCO, to name but a few (Whiteley, 1969; Stabler, 1969; Furley and Watson, 1978; The Ominde Commission, 1964; Sheffield 1973; Leo 1984). Contributing to the debate, Ngugi wa Thiong'o says that in the 1950s, during and after the State of Emergency declared in Kenya to circumscribe the Mau Mau movement, the district education boards, which then had more control over education ensured that in Kenya, English became more than a language: "It was *the language*, and all the others had to bow before it in deference" (Ngugi, 1986, p. 11). It is against this background that A.A. Kazimi, at the head of a commission studying the state of Asian education in Kenya advocated that pupils learn Urdu, Gujerati and other vernaculars (and a) "... greater emphasis be placed upon teaching the English language," (Furley and Watson 1978, p. 245).

Commeting on this, Furley and Watson state that "he (Kazimi) saw little value in Swahili in spite of its wide use amongst the ... Africans of East Africa" as well as non-African peoples. However, the significance of the language in the environment was such that quite soon after the report on Asian education in East Africa "Swahili became an accepted subject (even though) the Cambridge syllabus (centered in England) dominated the curriculum". At about the same time, Elspeth Huxley, an author and "a former white settler, placed the learning of Swahili high on the list of educational priorities" in what Furley and Watson (1978) have termed a provocative chapter entitled "some suggestions for promoting inter-racial goodwill through education."

Kiswahili then took its first major step in education. It was not only taught in African schools but was also offered in European and Asian schools as an option to compete with Latin, German, Greek, Urdu and Gujerati (Stabler, 1969). English was more than ever in a category of its own as the dominant language in all the branches of the curriculum. It had become the medium of instruction as well as subject in the arts, general subjects and science departments (Stabler, 1969).

In describing his own primary education, Ngugi (1986) has given the reader further proof of promotion of Kiswahili. He says that one of the subjects he studied and was examined in at the end of his elementary school career was Kiswahili (Ngugi,1986). As McCrum, Cran and MacNeil (1986) report, "in the East African states (Kenya, Uganda, Tanzania), the lingua franca tends to be Kiswahili, but English is the main language of all secondary and tertiary education" (p. 319). These writers should have added that although in Tanzania Kiswahili has been the language of instruction in primary school and to some extent in high school since 1968, English is still the language of instruction in Kenya at that level and above (Killam, 1984).

Some changes that were introduced include: (a) making Kiswahili an examinable subject from primary through high school to the university; (b) it was declared as the national language by the government in the early 1970s, although the official language remained English (Sheffield, 1973). Nevertheless, even though the government introduced Kiswahili as the national language, it was noted that the practical issue arising from the introduction of Swahili as the medium of instruction at the primary level are formidable, (Sheffield, 1973, p. 95). All these blocks were being erected in the way of Kiswahili's possible final triumph despite mounting evidence that its real influence was growing by the day and, in fact, the government could not do without it. As Leo (1984) reports:

> a government campaign to promote Swahili - *the only language virtually everyone speaks in Kenya* (italics added) - as *lugha ya taifa*, the national language, had done much to remove the stigma of inferiority that the European community had sought to attach to it. *In 1983, 'Swahili was spoken more and better than it had been a decade earlier.* (Italics mine) (p. 171).

While the government stance on the matter must be appreciated, it does not take away the fact that every government-sponsored commission from the colonial era to date has offered nothing short of hindrance to Kiswahili's triumph over English as the language of instruction in Kenya. The most significant of these education commissions after the State of Emergency are the Prator-Hutasoit report of the late 1950s, which led to the introduction of English as the medium of instruction from the first grade of primary school, and the Kenya Education Commission (the Ominde Report) of the early 1960s which confirmed the recommendations of the Prator-Hutasoit report on the subject (Stabler, 1969). All subsequent commissions and reports have done very little to change this state of affairs.

In spite of all the bottlenecks and hurdles that, through the years, have impeded the growth and development of Kiswahili in the Eastern African region, there is growing evidence indicating that its eventual triumph over the European languages may be imminent. Roscoe (1977) says:

> *Swahili has penetrated deep enough into East and even Central Africa for it to appear as a genuine alternative to English* (italics added). Rising along the coast of Kenya and Tanzania ... Swahili has spread inland through Kenya and Uganda, across Tanzania, into Zaire, Mozambique, (Northern Zambia, Southern Somalia) and even deep into Malawi, where it can be heard among the moslem communities of lakeshore towns like Karonga, Mangochi, Nkhota-khota, and Nkata Bay. According to (the late) Professor W.H. Whiteley, *Swahili is now poised to emerge as Africa's most dynamic modern language* (p.2).

As a matter of fact, in neighbouring Zambia, the story of Kiswahili is, similarly, encouraging. Kashoki (1978) reports that Zambia's national census of 1969 revealed that there were 7,495 native Kiswahili speakers in that country. The distribution of these speakers is described thus: "in Chiefs Mushili's and Chiwala's areas in the Ndola District, and ... close to the Zaire border, near Chienge in the Kaputa District. Several villages of Swahili speakers can be found in Chief Nsama's area in the Mporokoso District" (Kashoki, 1978, p.14).

Given the population trends in Africa since 1969, and more precisely after the attainment of independence, the Kiswahili-speaking population in Zambia can be expected to have at least doubled. As such, Kiswahili can be rated as a major minority language in that country.

References

Furley, O.W. & Watson, T. (1978). *A History of Education in East Africa*, Nok Publishers, New York.

Kashoki, Mubanga E . (1978) "The Language Situation in Zambia". In Sirarpi Ohannessian & Mubanga E. Kashoki (eds), *Language in Zambia*, International African Institute, London.

Killam, G.D. (ed) (1984). *The Writing of East and Central Africa*, Heinnemann, Nairobi.

Leo, Christopher (1984). *Land and Class in Kenya*, University of Toronto Press, Toronto.

McCrum, R., Cran, William & McNeil, Robert (1986). *The Story of English*, Elizabeth Sifton Books, Viking Penguin Inc., New York.

Ngugi, wa Thiong'o (1986). *Decolonising the Mind*, Heinemann Kenya, Nairobi.

Roscoe, Adrian A. (1977). *Uhuru's Fire: African Literature East to South*, Cambridge University Press, London.

Sheffield, James Rockwell (1973). *Education in Kenya: A Historical Study*, Teachers' College Press, New York.

Stabler, Ernest (1969). *Education Since Uhuru: The Schools of Kenya*, Wesleyan University Press, Middletown, CT.

Whiteley, Wilfred H. (1969). *Swahili: The Rise of a National Language*, Methuen and Co., London.

Chapter Three

Kiswahili: A Language Steeped in Controversy

Arguably, Kiswahili has been and still is one of the most controversial languages in Africa ever since colonialism consolidated control over the East African region. It has progressively earned fanatically uncompromising detractors as well as emotion-charged ardent supporters.

It will be noted that even though the identity of the language has been settled (as every reputable linguist and scholar agrees that it belongs to the Bantu cluster), its origin is still a subject of discussion and much dispute as some of its fine qualities, such as its vocabulary, particularly those lexical items that are known to originate from other languages, are perpetually being used to question its Africanness.

For decades, it has experienced resistance against its advancement as a possible language of wider communication nationally, regionally, and even continentally. Suggestions that it be considered as English's alternative in the role of instructional medium have been met with amusement at best and shock at worst.

The Arab-Descent Theory

There have been a number of "sound" reasons advanced against Kiswahili's adoption at any wider level. One of them is that Kiswahili is as foreign as the languages of the former colonialists, for, it has been argued, it was brought to these parts by Arabs at some unknown time; thus it is merely relatively older. In this light, Kiswahili is viewed as either Arabic, or an Arabic dialect. One prominent personality in this camp is Chinua Achebe, the reknowned Nigerian writer. This view is, however, fast losing its credibility, for no concrete historical facts have been so far unearthed to support it. It has further been refuted by the fact, supported by vast amounts of linguistic research, that Kiswahili does not resemble any of the Arabic dialects or even the known Afro-Asiatic languages in Africa, namely: Amharic, Hausa and Somali, which share features with the semitic languages - Arabic and Hebrew (Akmajian, Demers, Harnish, 1984).

Great amounts of evidence affirm the conviction of linguists from all over the world, who have ventured into the study of Kiswahili, as to where the language belongs. Polome, an American linguist, for example, has said:

> Swahili is a Bantu language, i.e. it belongs to the vast family of languages spoken south of a line stretching from the slopes of Mount Cameroun to the Northern shores of Lake Victoria, and thence towards the Coast, to Meru on the eastern slopes of Mount Kenya (and farther south, embracing the southern group [Zulu, Xhosa, Shona etc.] (Polome, 1967, p. 13).

Derek Nurse, a British linguist, has been more specific, placing Kiswahili within the broad umbrella group, North Eastern Coastal Bantu, in the Sabaki family, which includes two other Kenyan language groups: Mijikenda and Pokomo (Spear, 1978). Spear's ealier view, however, contends that Kiswahili might have evolved as a pidginised language embracing Bantu and Arab/Shirazi elements some time in the first half of the First Millenium A.D. at a place to the south of Somalia which was later known as Shungwaya (Spear 1978). Unfortunately, Spear does not give concrete evidence to support this contention save that Kiswahili does not share the tonal quality that seems to characterise most Bantu languages. In fact this is not a new linguistic breakthrough. Earlier, Polome (1967) noted the same. He was categorical in stating that "Bantu languages are tone languages" (p.14), but adding, nevertheless, that "Swahili has, however, lost this very important characteristic of Bantu, and this loss may be one of the most significant consequences of its presumable original development from a 'dialanguage' (Polome, 1967, p.14).

While the linguists' concern with or confoundment at this apparent anomally vis-a-vis wider Bantu norms may well be appreciated or even understood, it does not constitute enough evidence to disqualify Kiswahili from its Bantu family roots, because there has not been enough research proving beyond any doubt that *all* Bantu languages from Cameroun to South Africa are tonal. Furthermore, there is enough evidence to show that languages lose and/or gain new features when they come into contact with new languages and cultures. Polome (1967), has cited the southern Bantu languages (Zulu, Xhosa, etc.) which have a high number of consonant phonemes ... due to overlapping with the phonemic system of Khoi-san languages - which are non-Bantu (p. 13). Some of these phonemes are the click sounds which the Southern African languages do not share with the rest of the Bantu mega-group. Kiswahili itself gained the (X) phoneme as in *Khabari* (news), the (γ) phoneme as in *ghadhabu* (annoyance), the (ɟ) phoneme as in *dhahabu* (gold) and the (θ) phoneme as in *thabiti* (firm) from Arabic.

To understand what may have happened to some Kiswahili's probable original Bantu features as it was swayed by influences from other languages, one needs to consider what happened to other languages that went through similar historical changes. Of today's well-known modern languages, English is the best example. As with Kiswahili, English lost and/or gained novel features from a whole barrage of linguistic influences. It, for example, lost its (γ) Germanic phoneme in such words as enough, rough, bough etc., so that even though the spelling of these words indicates a vestigial phoneme, the actual sound is lost in pronunciation. The same can be said of the word-initial (k) sound in such words as "knight" and "knife" which is produced in other

Germanic languages such as German, Dutch and Danish. On the other hand, English gained important sounds such as (ž) as in the word *leisure* from the French.

It may thus not be linguistically expedient to start making claims and/or counterclaims on the possible origin of Kiswahili and/or its qualification in any group with evidence as scanty as that of tone. What should be taken into great consideration is the syntax; i.e. what has qualified Kiswahili into the Bantu cluster is it's indisputable Bantu structure, not the other relatively superficial features. Structure is what has retained English in the Germanic fold in spite of the collosal influences from all the languages of the world that it has historically brushed shoulders with.

Concerning Semitic Claims

It can be observed that the claim that Kiswahili is an offshoot of Arabic is quite illogical. This is becuase it cannot be derived from the semitic family and be at the same time purely Bantu in its structure. If the semitic theory had any credence, the language could at least have some lingering Arabic structural features, even after centuries of interaction with Bantu languages, as the Afro-Asiatic African languages referred to earlier do indicate.

Pidginisation Claims

(a) As a pidgin (a mixture of Arabic and Bantu), Kiswahili's syntax could be ruled by that of the superior language. Such is the case with all known pidgins and creoles; for example those of West African and the Carribean-Latin American regions, which are structurally, and even lexically, dominated by English.

(b) Again, as a pidgin, Kiswahili could have either more or at least half the lexical items of the superior language. Instead, it has been established that 60% of

Kiswahili's lexicon is Bantu, 30% is Arabic and about 10% is English, Portuguese, Persian, Indian and other non-Swahili Bantu (Mbaabu, 1978). Since Arabic is presumed to be the superior of the supposedly two component parts of Kiswahili, the language would be more semitic lexically than Bantu; or Arabic could at least claim half of Kiswahili's lexicon. This, however, is not the case; yet even if it were, Kiswahili could still be disputed as an Arabic or Afro-Asiatic language due to its untempered Bantu syntax. This is the case with English, which is only 20% Germanic lexically; but being syntactically more Germanic, it has been undisputed as a member of this group. It has never been listed among the Romance family of languages even though the largest percentage of its vocabulary (approximately 60% or more) has been either borrowed or derived from this family.

The Hybrid and Impoverished Vocabulary Theories

It will be observed that the latest onslaught against Kiswahili by its detractors is that it is a hybrid language in as much as it has a large Arabic vocabulary. And because it lacks important technological terms, it has been forced to borrow words from English, something that has been viewed as a weakness and not strength. The contention is that Kiswahili cannot stand on its own but, rather, has to depend on loans from other languages.

No one has ever disputed the fact that by far the greatest influence on Kiswahili has been its lexical borrowings. Scores of linguists have unearthed overwhelming evidence to prove this. Polome (1967) mentions several languages from outside Africa that influenced Kiswahili in varying degrees lexicologically. Of significance among these languages are Portuguese, Persian (introduced through Arabic, as the Arab settlers from Oman and Hadhramaut had been strongly influenced by Persian elements) (Polome, 1967, p. 11), and Indian; ... German to some extent. By far the most profound influences cited by Polome (1966), however, are Arabic and English.

Of the relationship between Kiswahili and Arabic, Polome (1967) says that the former" has been enriched in its own vocabulary by the influx of innumerable items of culture connected with Muslim civilisation" (p.11). This view is supported by Mbaabu (1987). However, it is English, and not Arabic, that has the greatest impact on Kiswahili in its recent development. This development is described with clarity by Polome (1967) who says that "the influence of English, with the new institutions and products of civilisation brought in by the British, has considerably enlarged the vocabulary, stuffing it with innumerable loans" (pp. 12-13). Even so, both the great influences and the minor ones have not altered the Kiswahili identity and place among the known and accepted families of languages. He further says that, in spite of even the latest pervasive influence on Kiswahili by the English language, "Swahili remains, as it did when it was similarly exposed to overwhelming Arab influence, *a strictly Bantu language* in its structure" (p.13) (italics added). One finds this view legitimated in a most unequivocal statement by Nurse and Spear (1985):

> Linguists have shown... Swahili is clearly an African language closely related to the Bantu languages now spoken along the northern Kenya and Somali coast, and... it has acquired much of its extensive Arabic vocabulary only in the last few centuries (pp. 5-6).

Nevertheless, the authenticity of Kiswahili has not been judged on the evidence of structure alone. As seen above, all sorts of linguistic features have been minutely scrutinized to find a properly fitting definition of the language. Phonology has been unconvincingly used against such authenticity. Syntactic structure has, quite contrary to expectations, gone to prove that it is, indeed, authentically Bantu. Nonetheless, lexicon has not helped much in shielding it from the accusation that it is a hybrid. It is the borrowing of lexical items from other languages to enrich itself that has rendered Kiswahili easy prey to detractors.

Accusations levelled at Kiswahili have been based on three grounds:

1) That it has diluted its traditional composition within the Bantu context.

2) That by borrowing from other languages, it has clearly proved that it is a weak language that lacks vocabulary and has thus had to rely on other languages to give it some semblance of sophistication.

3) That in spite of the heavy borrowing, Kiswahili still lacks the sophistication that is required to meet well-rounded communication requirements in today's super-sophisticated world where science and high-tech reign supreme. In Kenya, the yardstick against the background of Kiswahili's supposedly lack of sophistication has always been its traditional arch-rival in status, English, which is viewed as naturally the most appropriately suited to carry the heavy load of all human communication.

Comparison with English

It is necessary, at this juncture, to draw a comparison between Kiswahili and English not only because the two are the main contenders for status in Kenya - and frequent comparisons have always been made to justify Kiswahili's underdog position - but also because of English's undisputed greater sophistication, as well as Kiswahili's apparent hybridisation. In other words, the question here is whether a language can achieve the level of sophistication that English has proudly achieved by merely depending on its own potential from within its traditional skeletal boundaries. If this turned out to be the case, then Kiswahili's hybridisation would certainly be a liability or, in other words, a fair case against it.

Looking at the issue from another angle, there is the observation that once a language focuses its attention inside itself and closes the gates to all external influences, it faces the danger of digging its own grave. This is the manner in which the one-time world-conquering "stately" Latin, the once "universal medium of the written word" is alleged to have found its demise. In this case, Kiswahili's *focus-out* would account for its resilience and its eventual survival despite the strong attacks from varied, influential quarters.

The Epitome of Hybridisation

As stated earlier, English is only 20% Germanic (its parent cluster) while "80% ... of its teeming vocabulary... is foreign-born" (McCrum, Cran McNeil, 1986, p, 47). In comparison, Kiswahili is obviously severely starved; it has been stiffly conservative indeed in its willingness to *focus-out*.

A rejoinder will be made here to the effect that, while Kiswahili has been ridiculed for having such a "huge" foreign presence within its ranks (in reality severely insignificant, comparatively), a factor viewed as its main weakness, English has been hailed for precisely the same reason; that is, accepting as part of its milieu such an unashamedly gigantic foreign presence. McCrum, Cran, and McNeil (1986) have said that "it is the enormous range and varied source of this vocabulary, as much as the sheer numbers and geographical spread of its speakers, that makes English a language of such unique vitality" (p. 47). Such was already the view in the 16th Century when Sir Thomas Elyot, who apologetically introduced foreign words such as *education, dedicate* and *maturity* into the English language and popularised them, justified "borrowings from the Latin" as being "the necessary augmentation of our language" (McCrum, Cran, McNeil, 1986, p. 93).[35]

Even though the question of hybridisation of English has, apparently, not been the main worry of scholars of English language and linguistics, particularly in recent times, it seems to be one of the issues worth commenting about. For example, in the 19th Century, the English novelist Daniel Defoe felt pressed to define English as "your Roman-Saxon-Danish-Norman English" (McCrum, Cran, McNeil, 1986, p. 51) quite obviously not without a twinge of irony. Yet a century later, we do not notice any suggestive ironical note in McCrum, Cran and McNeil's tone when they gloat upon English's hybridisation, seeking to enlighten us on its roots, growth and development, at the same time. On hybridisation, the trio have further said: "English... is such a hybrid (of old Norse, German, Latin and Norman French) that it is peculiarly susceptible to pidginisation" (p. 45). They have described the language's roots and development as follows:

> Its roots are so varied Celtic, Germanic (German, Scandinavian and Dutch) and Romance (Latin, French and Spanish) - it has words in common with virtually every language in Europe: German, Yiddish, Dutch, Flemish, Danish, Swedish, French, Italian, Portuguese and Spanish. In addition, almost any page of the *Oxford English Dictionary* or *Webster's Third* will turn up borrowings from Hebrew and Arabic, Hindi-Urdu, Bengali, Malay, Chinese, the languages of Java, Australia, Tahiti, Polynesia, West Africa and even from one of the aboriginal languages of Brazil (McCrum, Cran, McNeil, 1986, p, 47).

Borrowing as Strength

English, then, is a language whose outstanding nature is its readiness to borrow with minimum restriction. Its fundamental lexical feature is the loan component, which is greater than its root component.

The language's main strength is its richness in vocabulary. McCrum, Cran and McNeil (1986) have exercised little circumspection in declaring that "of all the world's languages (which number some 2,700) it [English] is arguably the richest in vocabulary" (p. 19). Astonishing statistics reveal that the "... *Oxford English Dictionary* lists about 500,000 words, and a further half a million technical and scientific terms remain uncatalogued" (McCrum, Cran, McNeil, 1986, p. 19). English is still borrowing today from every corner of the world. American English has borrowed words like *wigwam, pretzel, spook, depot* and *canyon* (McCrum, Cran, McNeil, 1986, p. 235) from such diverse sources as American Indian, German, Dutch, French and Spanish. From Kiswahili, English has borrowed *safari* (trip, adventure) and *Bwana* (Lord, master, sir, male, husband). Recent borrowings from U.S.S.R. are *perestroika* (restructuring) and *glasnost* (openness) which owe their introduction and popularisation to Mikhael Gorbachev, the charismatic 1980s Soviet leader and his 20th Century revolution, plus the dynamic American media. This century, English has also had to resort to its ancient mentors, Latin and Greek, to augment itself, borrowing such words as *video, television* and *synthesizer* (McCrum, Cran, McNeil, 1986, p. 95).

With such staggering statistics, there can be no doubt that today English is an ultra-powerful language, but neither can there be any doubt, with all the available evidence, that its power is heavily foreign-based. What is most astonishing, therefore, is not the sheer size of the million-plus vocabulary count, which is truly amazing. It is rather the fact that English is still regarded as a Germanic language, in spite of the heavy tilt in its balance in favour of the foreign component of its cumulative lexicon. Of further significance is the fact that it has lost some of the structural features that most Germanic languages share (McCrum, Cran, McNeil, 1986). Ostensibly then, it is the fact that the language has retained the most central Germanic features, losing only the superficial ones, that has maintained it in its parent fold. It would, therefore, be linguistically honest to expect that when another modern, living, vibrant language such as Kiswahili is put to the scales, the same gauge be used in arriving at its most appropriate and deserving valuation.

The might of English and the strength gained from borrowing may well be fully appreciated when comparison is made vis-a-vis other European languages which have either sought to preserve their cultural purity by resisting loans or else have not had the global adventures and experiments that English has had or been exposed to. Two such other adventurous languages, German and French, can only credit themselves with dehydrated vocabulary counts currently standing at 185,000 and 100,000 respectively (McCrum, Cran, McNeil, 1986) with no hope of gaining expansion of any respectable size in the foreseeable future. Thus, apparently, the best method to lexical growth is not to *focus-in* but to *focus-out*. In light of this, Kiswahili's tentative borrowing should not be viewed negatively but positively. By the same token, for Kiswahili to expand, grow, maintain its vibrance and compete effectively with the metropolitan languages, thus winning for itself more prospects of replacing them, it should intensify its borrowing campaign, acquiring more loan words for itself with virtually no restriction placed in the way of such a campaign.

Borrowing in Kiswahili

Some borrowing has been advocated by quite a number of Kiswahili enthusiasts. The problem, however, has been that these enthusiasts are in different camps which often disagree on the format of borrowing that should be adhered to when developing the language. At times these disagreements have been so intense that the language has had to rely on the sheer speed of historical events and the users' needs, to develop itself, necessarily by-passing the wrangling scholars and their disciples in the process. A good example is President Nyerere's introduction of the Kinyamwezi words *bunge* (Parliament) and *ikulu* (State House) into the language while Kiswahili experts at the University of Dar es Salaam and around the country were busy racking their heads in search of the most appropriate words. Another example is the volume of technological items that Kenyan, Tanzanian and Central African Kiswahili grassroot users found themselves quite unconsciously absorbing into their language from English without waiting for approval from linguistic experts. The users' needs plugged the words into the language, and before they knew it, the scholars were themselves using them.

The "Jungu Kuu" Camp

The introduction of non-Swahili Bantu words into mainstream Kiswahili has, quite expectedly, not been acceptable to experts from within the Kiswahili community (known by their organisational title *jungu kuu*, literally "big pot", meaning there are always food crumbs in the big pot (one will always get something to eat)). These experts include Ahmad Sheikh Nabhany, a Lamu-born Mombasa resident and a committed, resourceful Kiswahili scholar.

The *jungu kuu* clique argues that there are enough words in Kiswahili to cater for all its needs in a changing world; only that such terms are scattered among its 15-plus dialects. Nabhany gives as an example four different denotative descriptions of "finger" in four dialects of Kiswahili, namely: *kidole* (Zanzibar dialect - Kiunguja), *chanda* (Mombasa dialect - Kimvita), *kijaa* (Lamu dialect - Kiamu) and *kinwe* (North Kenya Coast dialect - Kitikuu). The argument is that Kiswahili's full potential has not been exhaustively exploited from among all its older dialects; and that all the talk of presumed inferiority of the lexical capacity of the language has been based on overdependence on *Kiswahili sanifu* (standard Swahili), the youngest (just over two centuries old) of the dialects and, indeed, severely limited in most fundamental ways.

The *jungu kuu* camp, hence, advocates growth from within. Its foremost spokesman, Nabhany, would be happier if for example the words *jumbe* (or *yumbe* in Kiamu, and *gongwa* were used instead of the "foreign" endorsements *bunge* and *ikulu* (for parliament and state house respectively). While no one can dispute the authenticity of the words *jumbe* (*wajumbe* being parliamentarians) and *gongwa* in the context advocated by Nabhany, totally succumbing to an uncritical acceptance of *jungu kuu's* leadership could, in the long run, stunt Kiswahili's development.

The submission that the language is fully equipped from within its natural boarders may not exactly reflect the true picture on the ground as Nabhany himself unwittingly realises when he uses the Mijikenda word *sinya* (bore, boring, uninteresting) for lack of a better expressive Kiswahili word in that context. For that reason, we observe a significant development here, in which a recently purely Mijikenda word restricted in its Mijikenda environment is loaned into Kiswahili so that today *kusinya* (to bore) is acceptable in both Mijikenda and Kiswahili. Here is a case of the user's needs pre-empting experts' painfully slow strategies of endorsement.

Another crucial factor in the development of a transnational language like Kiswahili is its proximity and/or interaction with other languages and language users. It is, for example, an open secret that Kenyan Kiswahili has been structurally influenced by the neighbouring Mijikenda languages and vice versa (Spear, 1978). Now, while Kenyan Waswahili may love to deny any impact Mijikenda cultures and languages have had on Swahili culture and dialects, rather opting to favour the reverse as being the case, it has been firmly established, historically as well as linguistically, that the influences have been impressively mutual (Spear, 1978; Nurse, Spear, 1987; Salim, 1973; Kindy, 1972).

Apart from the Mijikenda languages in Kenya, it could well be argued that virtually every other language within the Kiswahili-speaking regions in East and Central Africa has influenced and been influenced by Kiswahili; particularly affected are those languages whose speakers (or any percentage of them) have been urbanised to some degree. Thus, some non-Bantu Africans of the Democratic Republic of Congo have influenced some brands of that country's Kiswahili (Whiteley, 1969). In Tanzania, some non-Swahili Bantus have brought some confusion in production of the glides (1), [r], so that in many words where these appear, they are produced interchangeably, sometimes colliding with native-Swahili pronunciations as with the word *ripuka* (explode, native Swahili), *lipuka* (Tanzanian/standard Swahili).

What is gaining more and more ground, however, is the introduction of non-ethnic Swahili structures into mainstream Kiswahili by East African writers who opt to write in the language and who may not necessarily be ethnic Waswahili. Henry Kuria of Kenya, who wrote the block-busting Kiswahili play of all time, *Nakupenda Lakini* contributed into mainstream Kiswahili usage of the word *ati* in his famous question *Ati nini?* (Say, what?) which is extracted straight from his native Gikuyu *Ati-kii*, a very pointed way of questioning. While native Waswahili make use of the word *ati*, it is never used in Kuria's context. We observe a very different usage of the word *ati* in the sentences: *Ati fulani amekufa?* (Is it true (*ati*) that so-and-so is dead?) and *Ataka kunioa ati* (He wants to marry me, of all presumptions) or *Ati ataka kunioa* (as a statement, meaning same as above, laden with ridicule ... Message: One idea he shouldn't have dared to entertain is marry me). This is typical native Swahili usage. Yet it is arguable that very few people, including mainstream

Waswahili experts, would today recognise Kuria's usage as authentically non-Swahili.

On the other hand, Kiswahili has introduced low-key technical words such as *karatasi* (paper) *panga* (cutlass), *jembe* (hoe), *debe* (8-gallon tin container) and numerous others in virtually all the Bantu and non-Bantu languages of East and Central Africa; not to mention that these lexical items have also inched their way into East and even South African English. No one interested in South African affairs after the release of Nelson Mandela failed to hear him exhort black people in Natal Province to take their guns, knives and *pangas* and throw them into the sea. It is highly doubtful that Mandela and other users recognise these words as loans from Kiswahili and not authentically English.

Some religious terms have quite coincidentally been borrowed by other languages from Kiswahili. Words like *shetani or shaitani* (devil) and *msalaba* (cross) may be so much part of the local vocabulary that their users may not be conscious of their true origin. For example, the world-famous Kenyan novelist, Ngugi wa Thiong'o, says of the title of one of his novels, *Caitaani Mutharaba-ini* (Kiswahili: *Shetani Msalabani;* English *Devil on the Cross*) that it is proof of Kiswahili's filial proximity to and concordial agreement with Gikuyu (Ngugi, 1986), perhaps not realising that Gikuyu got the loans from Kiswahili in the first place. Again, here is a case where users did not have to faithfully wait for scholars to pass judgement on the efficacy of these loans within Gikuyu, borrowed as they were from another language. The religious putsch, using the medium of Kiswahili first, then Gikuyu, dictated the infiltration of these terms into the newly loaned language. At another level, Kiswahili acquired them as loans from Arabic.

The "Wanamapinduzi" or Revolutionaries Camp

A second camp of Kiswahili enthusiasts will be referred to here as nationalists. The Tanzanian Kiswahili novelist Euphrase Kezilahabi is one of them. This group discourages borrowing from Arabic, advocating, Arabic instead, a new-old path, i.e. fishing for new loans from other African languages.

While one may not observe anything particularly wrong with such an advocacy, it will be noted that this path leads to the pitfalls in the *jungu kuu* - preferred method and will, as the latter, bring well-intentioned language developers to a *cul-de-sac*. The problem is immediately encountered as the unenviable undertaking of raking the field for words that correctly describe high-tech implements, and/or discoveries begin in earnest, just as the English language experienced. Furthermore, apart from unjustified ridiculing and/or abhorence of Arabic, this camp has not come up with one good reason why Kiswahili should not resort to its old mentor (Arabic) for new loans. English has found it incumbent to resort to Latin and Greek to enrich itself further. In any case, this clique sees nothing wrong with using English loans, as the newest Kiswahili dictionaries *(Kamusi ya Kiswahili Sanifu* and *Kamusi Awali ya Sayansi na Tekinolojia* from Tanzania) will show. Neither has the group expressed any loathing for the current large presence of Arabic loans already well-established as core lexical items of Kiswahili language.

The composition and approach of these two cliques may be described as purist. In the final analysis, their puritanical outlook may bring the whole struggle to a dead-end if their advocacy is given free rein to influence any number of people hungering for Kiswahili's genuine, fast development. While their sentiments and sincerity of intention may well be understood, their puritanism is definitely short-sighted, taking into account the fast pace of developments this century, and Kiswahili's own runaway flooding out of its East African coastal or even African borders.

The "Anglophile" Camp

A third camp comprises people who may be referred to as Anglophiles. This camp points at Kiswahili's loans as a sign of weakness. At every opportunity, this camp often challenges dedicated Kiswahili enthusiasts and scholars, with such taunts as: "You say that Kiswahili is self-sufficient (or as efficient as English), what is the Kiswahili word for motorcar?" The taunted party responds "*Motokaa*, of course!" (which is derived from English). "You see... even a simple concept such as motorcar - NO WORD IN KISWAHILI? What a language!" All this in between guffaws to emphasise the ridicule, as if to say: "Hurrah! *My* language (English) is the winner! I knew it!" Note that the people referred to here are Kenyan Africans, not foreigners.

These people would want to see Kiswahili have a word for *every* concept, idea, event or thing regardless of the native environment of the thing, event, idea or concept. Most of the people in this camp are not linguists or even "experts" in any language and they thus argue out of ignorance. They have little or no idea at all, for example, that the English they love so much at the expense of their own local language is totally dependent on loans. If challenged, they cannot say how English developed to such prominence. It is doubtful that half of them know that the seemingly very English words admiral, alcohol, algebra, elephant, gazelle, almanac, coffee and scores of others are borrowings from *Arabic*! There are of course the more serious borrowings - whole concepts, such as the numerals and zero, also from, of all languages... *Arabic*!

The English Way

A fourth camp of enthusiasts, which has not defined itself yet, advocates for Kiswahili the unabashed, indiscriminate, unlimited borrowing from all over the world, of the nature and magnitude of English, and possibly beyond.

The main premise of the camp is that no score is to be achieved in baring chests and unsheathing swords, solidifying determinations to resist the cultures, foreign and local, that interact with Kiswahili. There is absolutely no point in this kind of resistance. There is no point in spending several man-hours arguing as to whether the tiger, a non-native of Africa, should be Kiswahili-baptised *paka-milia* (big stripped-cat) or merely *taiga* - a Kiswahili spelling rendition of tiger, and a natural way of swahilising foreign words. If this method of swahilising words such as motor car (*motokaa*), lorry (*lori*), jail (*jela*), insist (*sisitiza*), responding to users' burning needs was good for Kiswahili a generation ago, why should it not be acceptable now? Why, all of a sudden, should Kenyans, Tanzanians, Congolese, Rwandese, Burundians, Comorians and all Kiswahili-speaking Africans at large be culture-sentively against it now?

When a genius such as Ahmad Sheikh Nabhany creates novel words like *runinga* (television), *mwengoya* (radio), *mangala* (microscope) out of what the concepts stand for, and as a result of actively interacting with his language and environment, all due credit should be given him, and the words should be immediately incorporated for normal, day to day use simply because they make sense. Nevertheless, the urgency of the need to develop Kiswahili is so great that we cannot wait for individual geniuses to create words.

In any case, this method runs the risk of bringing the language's development crashing against rocky walls when it comes to names of objects that are not found in certain environs. In cases where, say, a parent is required to explain to his or her child the nature and name of, for example, a bear, what explanation should the former give the latter? That strange bulky tundra animal on their television screen, what answer should the parent give to the child, given that the answer would be more meaningful if given in the native tongue - Kiswahili? How about the Japanese delicacy - *sushi* (raw-fish)? How about computer (currently swahilised *kompyuta*), menu (Swahilised *menu* not *menyu*), *fjord* (a Norwegian word that even the idolised English has no native equivalent for? It is just not possible to find a suitable word *in any single language* to denote or even connote everything and every event in this wide world which, as they say, has become a village.

The way for Kiswahili is to borrow heavily from other languages (local as well as foreign), without batting an eye; without entertaining or suffering any sense of remorse or misplaced guilt-conscience. This will not necessarily render Kiswahili unrecognisable as a Bantu language as has been severally claimed. Far from it. For, as long as the Bantu structure remains intact, no amount of alien lexical flooding will take away Kiswahili's Africanness.

On the other hand, the loan words Kiswahili needs to correctly describe new things and events in our severely altered environment will give it the punch needed to cater for continental and global linguistic requirements. Furthermore, borrowing will give it what it needs in order to appeal to national, regional, continental and global users. Already, and as stated earlier, enthusiastic students come to East Africa all the way from Ghana, Japan, Korea, Germany and the U.S.A. to study this language. These students, as representatives of different peoples the world-over, ought not to be disappointed by the fact that there are many things one cannot say in Kiswahili. Normally their motto is: "Say it in Swahili"; their paramount desire is to be able to say things in the language they have given a lot of their time and attention to acquire.

For us, the motto should be: Borrow, Swahilise the loan word, and let it adhere to Kiswahili (Bantu) phonological and morphemic systems. Give to Kiswahili the power it is already fast consolidating, one that it deserves, and it will crown itself with the glory of recognition among world languages of wide usage.

Of a Journal, Writers and New Coinages

At this juncture, it is recommended that a journal or journals be launched to publish any and all new coinages such as those of Nabhany mentioned earlier on in this chapter. The journal should also catalogue all the newly swahilised loan words from every corner of the world.

Another recommendation is that imaginative and creative writers be encouraged to coin new words which they will first use in their literature and afterwards the changes catalogued in the journal ready to be included in subsequent Kiswahili dictionaries. This is an ordinary way of developing a language that has always existed. It is known for a fact that Shakespeare created the word assassination (from assassin) and scores of others. Recently, Wole Soyinka, the renowned Nigerian playwright, poet, and Nobel Laureate followed Shakespeare's footsteps and his contributions have been properly catalogued. Writers like Sir Elyot, who was mentioned earlier on in this chapter, have also been known to introduce foreign words into their respective languages. Some terms introduced into the English language in this manner include *agile, capsule, habitual* (Latin), *catastrophe, lexicon, thermometer* (Greek) and also *encyclopaedia, explain, gravity,* etc. (McCrum, Cran, McNeil, 1986). During the Renaissance, newly created words such as *atmosphere, pneumonia* and *skeleton* entered the English language (McCrum, Cran, McNeil, 1986).

The writer of this book suggests below, some lexical contributions to the Kiswahili language in the hope that they will either supplement loan words already in use as synonyms or more significantly, fill the void where there is one, as in cases where English concepts such as *gravity* lack their equivalent in Kiswahili. It is suggested here that for the concept *mass* the words *sambao* and *tandao* (which may be loosely interpreted as expansive spread onto empty space) be used complementarily. For *gravity* the word *vutoti* (which may be interpreted as "the power that pulls down") be used. For volcano, the words *ripukochi* (explosion from underground), *vukutoti* (intense heat from underground), *vukuti* (intense heat from underground) and *volkeno* (already in use and swahilised from English) all be put into use. It is hoped that other lovers of Kiswahili will do the same.

References

Achebe Chinua (1975). *Morning Yet on Creation Day*, Heinemann, London.

Akmajian, Adrian, Richard A. Demers, and Robert M. Harnish (1984). *Linguistics: An Introduction to Language and Communication* (Second Edition). The Massachusetts Institute of Technology, Cambridge, Mass.

Kindy, Hyder (1972). *Life and Politics in Mombasa*, East African Publishing House, Nairobi.

Mbaabu, I. (1978). *Kiswahili Lugha Ya Taifa*, Kenya Literature Bureau, Nairobi.

McCrum, Robert, William Cran, and Robert McNeil (1986). *The Story of English*, Elizabeth Sifton Books. Viking Penguin Inc., New York.

Ngugi, wa Thiong'o (1986). *Decolonizing the Mind*, Heinemann Kenya, Nairobi.

Nurse, Derek, and Thomas T. Spear (1985). *The Swahili: Reconstructing the History and Language of an African Society, 800-1500*, The University of Pennsylvania Press, Pittsburg.

Polome, Edgar (1967). *Swahili Language Handbook*, Centre for Applied Linguistics, Washington, D.C.

Salim, Ahmed Idha (1973). *Swahili-Speaking Peoples of Kenya's Coast*, East African Publishing House, Nairobi.

Spear, Thomas T. (1978). *The Kaya Complex: A History of the Mijikenda Peoples of Kenya Coast to 1900*, Kenya Literature Bureau, Nairobi.

Whiteley, Wilfred H. (1969). *Swahili: The Rise of a National Language*, Methuen and Co., London.

Chapter Four

English as the Language of Instruction in Kenya

Background

Western education was first introduced in Kenya in 1848 by Dr. Ludwig Krapf, a German national in the service of the English Crown. Krapf's main aim was to train a few Africans who would then spread the 'good news' of salvation through Jesus Christ to their own kind. One year later, another missionary, Charles New, established another mission station a few miles from Krapf's mission center. New also started a school which followed a similar pattern to that of Krapf, particularly as regards to its main aim: to spread the Christian religion among the 'natives'.

These two missionaries set a precedence for education as more and more territory was consolidated on behalf of the British Crown. Separate mission groups established mission stations and schools. Expectedly, religion was the undisputed number one subject in these schools. Afterwards, however, other subjects such as English Language, English Literature, British History, Civics, Geography, Arithmetic, and Nature Study were introduced.

Initially, the missionaries preferred to teach almost all subjects of the curriculum, except English Language, in the languages of the natives, which were popularly known as vernaculars, especially in the lower grades. Religion, particularly, was to be taught and spread in the vernaculars which were thought to have some emotional appeal among their speakers. Later on, Kiswahili, which was the language that cut across ethnic boundaries, was preferred as the medium of instruction in upper grades of primary school. This occurred after the 1909 United Missionary Conference where delegates decided that the vernaculars would be instructional media in classes I to III, Kiswahili taking over as the sole medium of instruction in classes IV and V, whereas English would be optionally used as the instructional medium in these classes (IV and V) (Education Commission, Nairobi 1911, p. 405). Much later, English would become the undisputed language of 'higher thought'; that is, the language that would be used to teach more "sophisticated concepts". This automatically made it the language of instruction in high school.

In the beginning, this upgrading of English did not go unchallenged. Among those who did not feel that it was proper to raise the status of English at the expense of Kiswahili were Reverend John Arthur and the then Bishop of Mombasa who, in their memorandum to the Protestant Missionary Societies said:

> The Alliance while fully recognising the value of English in the higher training of natives cannot displace Kiswahili from its natural position as the lingua franca of the great mass of the natives of British East Africa (Education Commission 1919, p. 405).

It was not, however, until the 1940s when racially segregated schools became the main feature of the educational system in colonial Kenya, that debate on the language question took a serious turn. The system was designed to reflect the differences among the three prominent races so that there were separate schools for Europeans, Indians (popularly known as Asians), and Africans. In terms of quality, the European schools were the best, followed by those for Asians, while those for Africans were the poorest. Such a segregated system brought into sharp focus the question of language, particularly its instructional aspect which, allegedly, appealed to the emotions of the culturally diversified races.

The language of instruction in the European schools was to be English of course. The Asians were taught in Gujerati and/or Hindi in the first three grades and then English took over as the language of instruction from the fourth grade. The Africans received instruction in their respective vernaculars in the first three grades and then Kiswahili took over in the fourth grade to be replaced by English in the upper grades.

A combination of good (qualified) teachers, good school administration, appropriate methods of teaching, and the fact that funding per student was very biased in favour of European children (less than one percent of the population receiving 90% of the money), among other factors, led to European children performing a lot better than Asian and African children in examinations. At another level, the Asian children did better than the African children. This, in turn, created more opportunities for the Europeans to further their educational pursuits. Most of them got places in renowned British universities such as Cambridge and Oxford.

All these factors were eclipsed by the language factor when Africans started fighting for equal opportunity in education from the 1920s onward. The need to teach African children in English had initially been expressed by Europeans, particularly those who believed that Africans needed to be civilised in the European manner in order to appreciate western ways, and that the only medium that was suited for that task was a "civilised language" - English. The government, however, was reluctant to effect this for political reasons. Not much later, the push for English medium in African schools to start as early as first grade was made by the Africans themselves, believing that disparities in performance in examinations would be resolved. This push was intensified when the English medium was introduced in Asian schools from first grade.

At this juncture, it must be made clear that the Africans who led the battle were the same ones who had graduated from mission schools, and their perspective of civilisation and life generally was not radically different from that of their European 'adversaries'. Quite a number perceived deliverance in terms of stepping into the master's shoes, even linguistically. Africans were to be given instruction in English at all levels. By the time of the New Primary Approach, a study and recommendation concerning the direction Kenya would follow in education, Africans were already prepared for the big change. The remarks of Professor Prator of UCLA, called in to head the study, that the vernaculars were not equipped to handle sophisticated academic concepts (a view reiterated by Professor Ominde later on), met with applause instead of criticism from the Africans. At the time of independence in 1963, English was the language of instruction from the first grade of primary school to the highest level of the education structure.

The development of western education in Kenya can be summarised thus:

1. The missionary phase that began in the 5th decade of the 19th Century to the end of the first decade of this century. The emphasis was on saving the souls of Africans and so it had a very strong religious bias. Education pitted European civilisation against African culture. It emphasised the arts, more often than not down-playing African achievements. History, for example, started with the coming of the Europeans. Well into the first years of independence, the history curriculum consisted of a time-line of European penetration in Africa. Missionaries such as Dr. David Livingstone, navigators such as Vasco da Gama, explorers such as Grant, Samuel and Mary Baker, and government officials such as Portal and Owen were luminaries in history. African children around Mt.

Kenya, for example, were taught that *the first man* to see the mountain was Dr. Ludwig Krapf, the German missionary!

2. The Phelps-Stokes Commission, 1924, in which educationists from the U.S.A. recommended a Tuskegee Institute-type of education by which young Africans would be trained in tasks that required the use of their hands - a system that was said to have succeeded among American 'Negroes'.

3. The Beecher Commision, 1949, in which use of vernaculars for the first four years of primary school was recommended after which English would take over. Kiswahili was completely ignored.

4. The 1952 Binns' Report recommended that Kiswahili should be eliminated except where it was the mother tongue. Selected tribal vernaculars would be preserved. It was deemed necessary to eliminate Kiswahili because it was viewed as an obstacle to teaching "important" languages to African children, namely vernaculars and English.

5. The Prator/Hutasoit Commission, late 1950s, in which English was endorsed as the only language of instruction in all grades, significantly ushering in the so-called New Primary Approach, or English Medium Approach.

6. The Kenya Education Commission, 1964, in which national unity was to be the main aim of the newly independent country, taking care to preserve the different cultures of the different ethnic groups. Ironically, this commission, the first to be headed by an African (Professor Ominde of the then University of East Africa, Nairobi Campus) did not revise the language issue. This commission endorsed the Prator recommendations with a slight change. English was recommended to be the universal language of instruction in all schools in all grades whereas Kiswahili, the language seen as best suited to unify

the nation, would be a necessary subject. The vernaculars, on the other hand, were relegated to a more inferior status, with one period a week assigned to them.

7. The Gachathi Commission, 1976. Primary schools would consist of nine grades so that children graduating from these schools would be old enough to take care of themselves. Vocational education would be introduced to cater for primary school graduates who could not secure a place in high school. There was a slight shift from the recommendations of the Ominde Report with regard to the language question. English would be the language of instruction from the 4th grade up to university. Kiswahili would be an important subject in all primary and high school grades, having more weight in the fourth form examination, but still much inferior in status to English. The vernaculars would be the media of instruction in the "early grades of primary school".

8. The Mackay Commission, 1981, which recommended 8 years of primary education, 4 years of secondary education and 4 years of college education. English would continue to be the language of instruction, Kiswahili securely gaining a second language status; that is, becoming a compulsory, examinable subject in all grades of school, whereas the other ethnic languages would be languages of instruction among respective ethnic groups in lower grades of primary school. Kiswahili would, for the first time, be examined alongside other hitherto examined subjects in the national primary school examination at the end of 8 years of primary school.

It may be observed that post-colonial language policies have deviated very little from policies adopted during the pre-independence era. That mother tongues (including Kiswahili) have a place in the curriculum appears to be largely influenced by the 1950s UNESCO standpoint that children all over the world be instructed in their own languages in the first grades of primary school, rather than any deliberate change of policy and/or attitudes on the part of educational planners.

An argument may thus far be advanced to the effect that commissions, led as they are by people with some definite preferences of their own, may arrive at preconceived recommendations. In the present situation, the same observation may be made. That almost every one of these commissions endorsed English at the expense of Kiswahili and other mother tongues is no coincidence. It is rather more likely than not a result of dominant or lingering elitist attitudes; sort of "natural selection". The likelihood is that commissioners could approach the problem subjectively, nursing their own biases, motives and motivations and, in the process, harbouring preconceived notions of what is good for the citizenry at large. Such an approach, even with the best of intentions, eventually fails to meet its objectives.

Analysing a similar situation in regard to the former Portuguese colonies of Africa, Freire (1985) has observed:

> For many years, from childhood through adolescence, these very people who achieved liberation for their countrymen were marked by a socialisation process in which the colonisers would not recognise Creole as an autonomous and beautiful language. On the contrary, the colonisers had to convince the people that the only valid language was Portuguese. They always emphasised that what the colonised spoke was an ugly and savage dialect.... After centuries of hearing that Creole is ugly and not valid, people begin to believe this myth. I have heard many well-educated people in Africa tell me that Creole is not a language, that they have to maintain Portuguese because *it is a superior language* (italics added). I always used to tell them that their assessment of Creole is a form of reproducing the dominant ideology, that of the coloniser... (These) people stress that they need to advance technologically and scientifically because otherwise they jeopardise the struggle for liberation. It is as if the Creole language does not have all the pre-conditions to fulfil these

tasks, particularly in the modern sciences. None of this is true... this is false reasoning (p. 185).

Freire (1985) has expressed concern that if this kind of reasoning is given free reign to permeate and influence society, what will result is a "deepening (of) social class differences" (p. 184). He has further postulated that:

> In continuing to use Portuguese, there is yet another danger: eliticism. Since they are educated by the coloniser and are thus very fluent in Portuguese, only the politicians and their children are bilingual. Only powerful families succeed in the educational system. Children of these families are the only ones who excel in examinations and get good grades. They are the only ones who have access to science and technology. Thus, most children, the sons and daughters of peasants, will be excluded. And tomorrow the new generation of power will comprise only the children of the families in power today. (Freire, 1985, p. 184.)

The language question in Africa generally, as per above evidence, has always been, and remains an emotion-rousing one. It has always embraced other spheres of life such as politics, economics and culture, making it an issue closer to the hearts of those involved. It has hence been instrumental in defining their stand in the other spheres. It has created (or has always had the potential to create) divisions while on the other hand cementing relationships across such seemingly irreconcilables as race, social class and the like. However, where relevance of one language or the other in influencing the lives of the people at large has been the question, disagreement has been bitter and almost absolute.

In Kenya, such a disagreement appears to have always existed tamely, seething underneath, only recently making itself sharply felt in the views of a new class of educationists spearheaded by teachers of literature in the main. In September 1974, at a conference organised by University of Nairobi's

Department of Literature in conjunction with the Inspectorate of English in the Ministry of Education, the Literature teachers, headed by Eddah Gachukia (then a lecturer at the University) and S.K. Akivaga, recommended that:

> A clear programme of Swahili literature be introduced and be made compulsory in schools.
>
> Every language has its own social and cultural basis, and these are instrumental in the formation of mental processes and value judgements. *Whereas it is accepted that we use English and will continue to do so for a long time to come* (italics added), the strength and depth of our cultural grounding will ultimately depend on our ability to invoke African culture in a language that is closer to it. *Swahili has a major and increasing role to play in Kenya, and needs to be given greater emphasis than it has hitherto been accorded* (italics added). An immediate step that should be taken to fulfil this aim is that adequate numbers of Swahili teachers should be trained (cited in Ngugi, 1986, p. 99).

There is a parallel between this stance and that of Freire (1985) who, commenting on the predicament of former (African) Portuguese subjects with regard to the question, says:

> I think you will agree that it would be very foolish... to cut themselves off completely from the Portuguese language, just because it is the language of the coloniser. To renounce totally the positive aspects of the Portuguese culture makes no sense.... *The question that needs to be asked is how to activate and formalise the use of the African languages so they can gradually replace the coloniser's language in such fields as economics, politics and finance* (p. 183) (italics added).

Thus it would appear that the chances of European languages eclipsing African languages are slim indeed. From the observation above, the trend tends to favour a replacement of the foreign languages with those indigenous to the African continent, even if such an objective may or should take years to realise. It seems that, whatever the appeal of the European languages to the planners (whether emotional, psychological or class based), the very evironment (geographical, cultural, social, political, educational and otherwise) will favour indigenous languages in their battle against foreign languages. It is by this very token that in spite of real as well as imagined discouragement against those championing the cause of indigenous languages and the cause itself, the debate has always surfaced, re-surfaced and persisted with more and more fervour as years come and go. In Kenya especially, the issue has adamantly refused to just die off as indicated by the most recent sentiments expresssed by a number of educationists from East and Southern Africa.

At a Nairobi conference attended by 22 ministers of education from the region (in November 1989), African states were "... called upon to drop the use of foreign languages in schools and instead adopt mother tongues as medium (sic) of instruction" (*Daily Nation*, November 24, 1989). The meeting was sponsored by the World Bank, UNICEF, UNDF, and of most significance, UNESCO, which has espoused the use of mother-tongues for instructional purposes for decades; Kenyan personalities who have unswervingly held the mother-tongue banner prominently featured at the meeting. One such personalilty is Eddah Gachukia, currently a consultant with UNESCO, who, reading the conference recommendations, is quoted as having said:

> ... foreign languages *had been identified* (italics added) as a major stumbling block in providing education effectively especially in rural areas...The languages were identified as one of the factors behind the high school drop-out rate. Foreign languages inhibit learning and kill our culture (*Daily Nation*, November 1989).

This sentiment was echoed a few days later by another seasoned proponent of mother tongue instruction, Chris Wanjala, an Egerton University Professor. The *Daily Nation* newspaper of December 9th 1989 gives the following report of Chris Wanjala's dissatisfaction with the language question in the country today:

He said the study of African literature in high schools has been replaced by '... "Communication skills". Under this programme, it has been ensured that, the myriad of mother tongues in Kenya do not "interfere" with the spoken language of the students. He said, students spend all their time practising communication skills, adding that the purpose of the curriculum is to produce a generation of Kenyans who speak uniformly. He said this is not done even in the United Kingdom, where spoken English is greatly influenced by local dialects and accents. Prof. Wanjala further said, "Kenya will lose the great beauty of its languages and the students stand no chance of understanding their culture and heritage". (*Daily Nation*, December 9, 1989.)

Apparently, as long as English is the language of instruction and indigenous languages continue to be spoken by the various ethnic groups in Kenya, the language question - especially the instructional aspect, will continue to be among the top, favourite, hotly debated issues. If but a tiny fraction of the claims made by Gachukia and Wanjala - among others - has a grain of substance, then the nation faces problems that critically translate directly to the way it will develop and define its uniqueness vis-a-vis other countries - both developing and developed. For it is well known that great devotion has been made to education judging from the size of the annual votes. Equally significant is the fact that preservation of culture, indigenous languages and ethnic identity has been one of the favourite themes of education planners in Kenya beginning with the ground-breaking 1964 Ominde Commission.

The English Language Question Globally

The English language question has been viewed as a uniquely African problem. But this is a misconception (consider the "Tower of Babel" theory) as a brief cross-sectional survey shows how other peoples in a number of former British colonies, the U.S.A. and Britain itself have reacted in regard to English. This and other areas will be looked into in this section.

Starting with the largest Anglophone countries in terms of number of speakers and sheer geographical size, it will be observed that the U.S.A. has a problem with the English language. In the first place, English is not the national language of the U.S.A. - in any case, it has not been passed by an act of Congress to be such. In the second place, English is not the only language spoken in the U.S.A. In other words, U.S.A. is not monolingual. There are the languages of the native Americans, for instance. There are also other less well-publicised languages such as the Louisiana Creole, a hybrid of English, French, African and Native American languages. It is spoken as a mother tongue by a number of native born Louisianans. For them, English is an acquired, second language. Then there is Gulag, spoken by African Americans in some islands off the Carolinas Coast. But by far the language with most speakers, and a fierce contender in any position vis a vis English, is Latin American Spanish.

Latin American-Spanish has really and firmly established a bilingual question in the U.S.A.; and because of it, all problems associated with a bilingual situation have made themselves felt by Educational planners and politicians who have been forced to address them.

Today, Spanish-speaking children, not only in such traditionally Spanish settled states as Texas, New Mexico and California, but also in inner-city Spanish areas within New York and Chicago for instance, have forced educationists to review conservative language policies. In such areas, children are taught in Spanish in the first grades, and gradually incorporated into English instruction. When Spanish is in use as the language of instruction, children are encouraged to speak in English. From a very early age, they are made to understand that one faces fewer problems getting a good job with knowledge of English. But by token of the mere fact of its existence and the number of its speakers, which are fast growing, Spanish has decisively stopped on the track any notions of an America "unified" by the English language. The tendency is towards diversity, not superimposed unity.

India

India, a country reputed to have more than 70,000,000 English speakers - a population larger than that of Britain - had an objective of eliminating English within a generation (McCrum, Cran, McNeil, 1985, p.332). This objective was stated by Prime Minister Nehru in 1947. Today, however, this objective has not been fulfilled and, as the population figure may suggest, the language seems to be thriving instead of withering even though the English speakers are a tiny minority in a country of more than 800,000,000 people. And even though it is spoken by such a vast number of people, English is not the language of instruction in most Indian states. Hindi, Punjabi and many other local languages are the languages of instruction.

The status of English in India is that of a model second language. "It is taught as a second language at every stage of education in all states of the country" (McCrum, Cran, McNeil, 1386 p. 322). It is likely to be the language of instruction in two states - Meghalaya and Nagaland where it is the state language (McCrum, Cran, McNeil, 1986 p. 322). The vast majority of its speakers are over-whelmingly from the educated, ruling elites (McCrum, Cran, McNeil, p. 322). English is also still the language used in examinations in the universities, conducts foreign affairs and opens the way to a "business career" (McCrum, Cran, McNeil, 1986 p. 332).

It is thus apparent that the Indians have not contravened the stated objective of UNESCO pundits on the question of mother-tongue instruction, except perhaps in the two states. The psychological turmoil, if not cultural, well-associated with teaching young children in a foreign language seems to have been deliberately taken care of in this large nation.

Britain

Britain has not been immune to battles with colonial languages. Two languages English battled against and won were Latin and French. At one time in Britain, French was the official language whereas Latin was the language of erudition. English, the indigenous language of England, had to be liberated from its "inferior" status by King Henry V who was the first English King to make use of it for his official correspondence (McCrum, Cran, McNeil, 1986 p. 85). King Henry also fought and defeated the French. To drive home his determination that English, and not French, be the official language of his nation, he "symbolically sent his messages to the French in English" (McCrum, cran, McNeil, 1986, p. 84).

However, as with the case of Kiswahili and other indigenous languages versus English in Kenya, in England, the mere endorsement of English by King Henry as the official language did not necessarily generate universal love of and/or respect for the language by all its native speakers. There was the usual fierce friction between those who, inspired by national pride, supported the decision with full-blown enthusiasm on one camp, while another camp preferred the language of erudition - Latin, and the language of the former rulers - French.

People in the second camp were Francis Bacon the poet, and Sir Isaac Newton the scientist, who are ironically known to have contributed a lot to the English language, culture and technology. Their contribution apart, Bacon and Newton preferred Latin to English. Bacon for one, is reputed to have declared that English would "play the bankrupts with books" (McCrum, Cran, McNeil, 1986 p. 92); whereas Newton is said to have found "most clarity in Latin" (McCrum, Cran, McNeil,

1986, p. 129). These two were not alone in this camp. It has been established that many other men (of learning) looked to French as a means to "purify our Native Language from Barbarism or Solecism" (McCrum, Cran, McNeil, 1986 p. 129).

Apart from King Henry, the other camp also won dutifully determined proponents; and this camp later succeeded in its centuries' old struggle. It would, however, appear that getting supporters was not a spontaneous process for this camp. Unequivocal support took a long time to consolidate. For example, it was not until the sixteenth century, a whole century after King Henry's decision, that people such as Roger Mulcaster openly made their stand in support of their national language, describing its merits visa-a-vis the dominant foreign languages of their time, namely: Latin and Greek. Mulcaster is recorded as saying:

> I honour the Latin but I worship the English ... But why not all in English, a tung of it self depe in conceit, and frank in deliverie? I do not think that anie language, be it whatsoever, is better able to utter all arguments, either with more pith, or greater plannesse, than our English tung is, if the English utterer be as skilfull in the matter, which he is to utter: as the foren utterer is .... It is our accident which restrains our tung, and not the tung itself, which will strain with the strongest, and stretch to the furthest, for either government if we were conquerers, or for cunning, if we were treasurers, not anie whit behind either the subtle Greke for couching close, or the statelie Latin for spreading fair. Our tung is capable, if our people wold be painfull (cited in Whiteley, 1969, p. 43).

The tone of this impassioned plea suggests a person on the defensive, forced by his love for his language to put it on the same pedestal as the "more superior" languages for the record, but fails to convey any conviction on the part of the proponent of actual belief in the real worth of the object of his love. The reader is more convinced by Mulcaster's apologetic inclination towards the languages he reveres but which he has to attack as necessitated by the situation.

Later generations did not have to feel as apologetic though. One of this camp's best known fighters was the Irishman Jonathan Swift who lived two centuries after Mulcaster. Swift not only fought for English, but also against the corruption of it. He fiercely advocated the use of "the proper form" of English. He was particularly appalled by "the chaos of English spelling" (McCrum, Cran, McNeil, 1986 p. 132).

The language question in Britain today has, in the main, been reduced to the Queen's English on one hand versus the dialects such as Cockney and influences of Irish and Scots on the other hand. The history of the battle is as old as the dialects and nationalities themselves and has involved such personalities as John Keats (the "Cockney poet"), Irish writers such as Spenser, Congreve, Swift, Sherridan, Wilde, Yeats, Synge, George Bernard Shaw, James Joyce, William Becket, among others, and Scottish writers such as Sir Walter Scott and Robert Louis Stevenson (McCrum, Cran, McNeil, 1985 p.163; 147).

West Africa

Elsewhere, Ghana lost the battle to completely eradicate the ethnic languages, filling the void with English. Kwame Nkrumah started this war as a means of dealing a blow to cultural diversity. Today, several Anglophone West African countries such as Nigeria, Cameroon, Ghana, Sierra Leone and Liberia have evolved their own pidgin English which is spoken transnationally and cross-ethnically. A significant feature in this development is that these countries lack one common language that may be spoken transnationally and/or cross-ethnically. In this context, English seems to have, so far, had no rival. This, however, is not the only reason why English has recorded success in this region.

As in the U.S.A. and Kenya, another angle to the issue seems to be strictly, that of bread and butter. This is clear judging from a statement by Sierra Leone's former President Siaka Stevens' that, "If you want to earn your daily bread, the best thing to do is to learn English. That is the source from which most jobs come" (McCrum, Cran, McNeil, 1986 p. 46). The "daily bread" factor also appears to be one of the most critical motivations in the battle for English instruction by Kenyan Africans in the 1940s and 1950s.

Singapore

In Singapore, a Prime Minister, Lee Kuan Yew, is known to have adamantly championed standard English. He was quoted as saying:

> There is this naive belief that because the language is English, therefore, it is not part of me, so I cannot learn to use it as well as an Englishman. This is utterly wrong.... We were fortunate in that quite fortuitously American technological and economic dominance coincided with our English heritage (McCrum, Cran, McNeil, 1986 p. 55-6).

Singapore faces the problem experienced in the West African countries. There are three major ethnic groups in that country - Chinese, Malay and Tamil - each guarding its cultural identity and language jealously. There is no common language spoken by all the ethnic groups except the newly emergent pidgin - "Singlish" which the chief minister was actively and openly fighting against, though all indications point to the fact that he was, even then, on the losing end of the battle.

Malaysia

In Malaysia, a country with a majority ethnic group, Malay, and strong minorities - Chinese and Indians — English was dropped as a language of instruction and as a second language in the entire education system. It was replaced by the dominant ethnic language - Malay. The status of English currently is that of a foreign language, offered in the Malaysian school system just as one of the several foreign language options, such as French, German and Japanese, among others. Consequently, Malaysians have lost their grasp on the English language and Malaysian students abroad have to learn the language before they can embark on their speicifc areas of study.

The Language of Instruction

Most of the examples discussed above tend to emphasise the political, cultural, social and instructional barriers blocking the imposition of an outside language (outside local cultures and environment) as the dominant medium of expression. Whether one is dealing with the resistant Spanish-speaking Americans, the nationalistic Britons, the Nehrus, or the developers of pidgins, all the way to the advocates of the use of local languages such as Kiswahili and other mother tongues (in Kenya), the emotion evoked is the same; rejection of what is considered foreign in favour of what those involved perceive as their own. On the question of the language of instruction, very strong views have been expressed; for example, that foreign languages inhibit learning and are a stumbling block to effective education. These views have the immediate effect of discrediting or even shattering the "higher thought" theory that has always been associated with them.

If foreign languages are indeed stumbling blocks, they cannot be expected to enhance learning. They are limited as facilitators of communication. They retard instead of developing thinking. In regard to the above views, any instructional, or educational problems of countries that use foreign languages as instructional media are of fundamental psychological and developmental significance and should thus never be ignored or given second priority consideration. They need to be thoroughly studied and coherently addressed.

Freire has addressed this problem in the following manner:

> The main problem is that these countries adopt Portuguese as the official language for technical, scientific, and political thinking. You have Cape Verdean children who have to learn geography, history, biology, math, and the social sciences in Portuguese. *This should be the task of the national language*, not the official language (italics added). This is like asking my children in Brazil to study the history of Brazil in English. You can see what a violation of the structure of thinking this would be: a foreign subject (such as English) imposed upon the learner for studying another subject. *If a Cape Verdean child has difficulties learning the Portuguese language, you can imagine how difficult it would be to learn other subjects in Portuguese* (italics added)(Freire 1985 p. 184).

In Kenya, we have quite a number of options at our disposal. We may either appeal to our national pride as the British did in the 15th century and replace the official language (English) with the national language (Kiswahili) as the language of instruction. Or we can adhere to the UNESCO call and teach our children using the mother tongues at least in the lower grades and, thereafter, decide where the national and/or the official languages will take over. Or we can develop our own pidgin as the West African and South East Asian countries have done. This, however, appears to be unlikely. A pidgin seems to develop where there is no common language.

In Kenya, Kiswahili has already occupied the position of common language. It is thus apparent that neither pidgin English nor its creole form is likely to develop in our particular linguistic environment. Instead, a kind of pidgin Kiswahili with a Swahili structure but embracing English vocabulary and those of other Kenyan languages has already evolved. This "language", known as *sheng,* has found its first literary user in the veteran populist writer David Maillu, better known as the author of *My dear bottle* and *After 4.30*. His new book, *Without Kiinua Mgongo* has been written in this "language".

Another option is to drop the English language altogether as Malaysia has done. The wisdom of this may be questioned on the basis of the trouble young Malaysians have, having to struggle with the language before beginning serious studies in universities outside Malaysia. Certainly, communication with English-speaking outsiders has been rendered difficult for Malaysians as a result of this decision. If anything positive is to be viewed from the decision, it is that it has further shattered the "language of higher thought" theory as Arabic did in the Arab world not many years earlier; thus rendering more and more irrelevant the highly disputed and utterly subjective age-old claim that there are inherently superior (or civilised) languages that stand out in majesty against inherently inferior (or primitive) languages.

Otherwise, as Freire has pointed out, it is not wise to drop a language just because it is a colonial language. Any language has many positive aspects to offer and people should not get rid of a language they already have access to just because they find the history of the language or some aspects of it, annoying or even degrading. On the other hand, Kenyans may find Freire's advice of gradually phasing out the colonial language (not drastically as in Malaysia), eventually replacing it with their languages, a reasonable compromise.

But Why Not All in ... Kiswahili?

An alternative that may appeal to many nationalists is not to gradually phase out English as a language of instruction, replacing it with the national language, but to define a suitable role for the other mother tongues in instruction; while at the same time retaining English as a subject in all levels of schooling as is the case in India. This will ensure that Kenyans learn their own subject matter in their own languages while retaining a language that has carved for itself a very prominent position in the world today. To be precise, Kiswahili should switch positions with English in instruction, and become a national language in the true sense while English retains no more than its official language status.

This would be the most logical thing to do in the light of the new, eloquently revealing evidence that Kenyan learners across the nation appear to understand Kiswahili better than English (*Daily Nation*, March 1, 1990; March 3, 1990; *Sunday Nation*, March 4, 1990).

The 1989 Fourth Form examination results, which indicated that there were mass failures in mathematics, sciences and English language (*Sunday Nation*, March 4, 1990, p. 2) and subsequent comments by the Ministry of Education and the Kenya Examinations Council officials, lend a lot of weight to this contention. Evidence shows that, while English was performed miserably, good performance was recorded in Kiswahili, history and government, christian religious education and agriculture (*Daily Nation*, March 1 1990 p. 6). It was further reported that "English was ... poorly performed.... many candidates could not spell or follow instructions and hence gave irrelevant answers. Many of them had not mastered basic grammar (*Daily Nation*, March 1, 1990 p. 6). The *Sunday Nation* of March 4, 1990 carried another report revealing that English "... had a mean score of 57.32 out of 200" (p. 2).

It should be noted here that English should not be completely eradicated, but rather be relegated to its true and deserving position in Kenya - that of a strong second language. The other indigenous languages of Kenya could be placed on the same instructional pedestal as the all-national language. This might reduce the magnitude of rivalry between Kiswahili and English but might unleash an even more fierce struggle between the former and the forty-odd ethnic Kenyan languages. Under such circumstances, we will have been led to face the greatest challenge of the idea of nationalism, unity, identity and national pride.

Logically, it ought to be clear to educational planners that learners may find it easier to grasp concepts in other subject areas if the language of instruction is easily understood than when the instructional language is itself difficult to understand as a subject. The need to come to terms squarely with this way of looking at the language issue is urgent because one more revelation of the overall performance in that examination was that, as the Kenya National Examinations Council put it, "candidates showed lack of understanding of the basic concepts" (*Daily Nation*, March 4, 1990, p. 4). It follows that, if the candidates could not understand the language in the first place, how could they be expected to make head or tail of the concepts expressed through that medium? Contrary to this, it would be expected that students would understand most of the concepts they found difficult to understand in English if the language of instruction were Kiswahili, which they understand easily.

In case the latter alternative (Kiswahili replacing English) is to be opted for by Kenyans, several suggestions offered below are helpful to school curricula planners:

1. The social sciences may be immediately taught in Kiswahili as has been since the beginning of education in Kenya in those areas where the language has had the greatest influence for centuries. There will be very little inconvenience felt across the nation since the language is spoken with ease and competence by the majority of Kenyans trans-ethnically, particularly among the young nationals at whom all educational planning should be directed.

2. Kiswahili could take over from the other mother tongues from lower primary onwards, replacing English as pupils move on to the next class, as

happened when implementing the 8-4-4 education system; that is, beginning with completely new groups.

3. Retaining English as the language of instruction in teaching science subjects until the social sciences approach has been proved effective and then gradually phasing out English in the natural sciences too, beginning from Primary Four upwards.

4. Retaining English at university level until the primary and secondary systems are complete and successful, then gradually doing away with English at this level too.

The whole exercise may start anywhere; from 8 years to 48 years to complete. The problem may be tackled at two levels simultaneously: namely primary on one hand, and high school/university on the other hand, thus, taking only 8 years. On the other hand, a bottom-up approach may be taken, starting from primary, all the way up to university; thus taking 16 years. Or the phasing out by subject, beginning with subjects that are within the closest experiences of the learners and moving further away from their immediate experiences. Or it may be based on subjects as well as levels (primary, secondary and university), thus necessitating lengthened phasing-out block periods of 8, 16, 32 and 48 years, making sure that whichever mode of phasing out is used, 48 years should be considered the maximum tolerated period of full implementation.

In short, in planning, we should consider not only the whims of the present generation, which has already reaped, or is in the process of reaping, from the old and present systems, but we should particularly take the interests of posterity into the greatest consideration. As the saying goes, "the present is in our hands but the future is not, and whatever we do now will expose us to the scrutiny and either sympathetic or unsympathetic, approving or disapproving judgements of future generations".

References

Daily Nation, March 1, 1990.

Education Commission (1919). *The Commission on Education in the East African Protectorate*, Nairobi.

Freire, Paolo (1985). *The Politics of Education*, Bergin and Garvey Publishers Inc., South Hadley, Massachussets.

Gachukia, Eddah (1989). In *Daily Nation* Nairobi.

McCrum, Robert, William Cran and Robert McNeil (1986). *The Story of English*, Elizabeth Sifton Books. Viking Penguin Inc., New York.

Ngugi, wa Thiong'o (1986). *Decolonizing the Mind*, Heinemann Kenya, Nairobi.

Sunday Nation, March 4, 1990.

Wanjala, Chris (1989). In *Daily Nation*, December 9, 1989, Nairobi.

Wanjala, Ellam Khalagai (1985). *Problems of Learning in a Second Language: A Consideration of the Problems that Kenyan Primary School Children Encounter when Learning in English with Special Reference to Mathematics.* An unpublished Masters' Thesis submitted to the University of London.

Whitely, Wilfred (1969). *Swahili: The Rise of a National Language.* Methuen and Co., London.

Wigginton, Eliot (1985). *Sometimes a Shining Moment: The Foxfire Experience,* Anchor Books, New York.

KISWAHILI:
THE RISE AND TRIUMPH OF AN INTERNATIONAL LANGUAGE

PART II

Chapter Five

Status of Kiswahili in East and Central Africa Within a Continental Context

Background

Kiswahili's rapid rise to prominence, from the second half of the 19th Century onwards in the East and Central African region and beyond, is a historical phenomenon that has impressed scholars and other interested parties of varied schools of thought. It is a matter that has captured the interest of sociolinguists, administrators, educationists, writers, anthropologists, geographers and historians alike.

The greatest tribute has been the short duration it has taken to spread across the length and breadth of such a large territory without the resources and backing that the metropolitan languages (e.g. English, French, Portuguese and even German) have for centuries, enjoyed. While English has the British Council, French has the French Cultural Centre(s) and German has the Goethe Institute(s), all powerful sponsors, Kiswahili has no equivalent in all the countries where it is spoken. The language, thus, depends on its natural appeal and governments' support where the latter spot the need.

This is a typical case of *Chema chajiuza, kibaya chajitembeza*, a Kiswahili saying which (in English) means a good thing sells itself while a bad one depends on the advertiser.

There have been heated debates on factors regarding the language's success. In the final analysis, however, people from different schools of thought generally seem to be in agreement about the influence of three factors: trade, religion, and politics.

Trade

It has been established that Kiswahili was spread inland by its coastal mother-tongue speakers who have been, for centuries, very adventurous entrepreneurs. The Waswahili were adventurous seafaring people who sailed as far away as Arabia and possibly India. As their literature suggests, while inland, they explored the interior of Tanzania going as far west as Eastern, Southern and North-Eastern Congo. Southwards, they reached Malawi, Zambia, Mozambique and Madagascar.

Whereas the available evidence does not show any significant traces of their language in Arabia and India (except in Oman where it was imported by East African dwellers not more than three decades ago, and Kathiawar, India, where a Kiswahili dialect described as *sidi* was imported by slaves from East Africa and is to this day spoken by descendants of these people there (Whiteley, 1969)) the full impact of Kiswahili, particularly as a second language owing its spread primarily to trade, is heavily experienced in Tanzania and the Democratic Republic of Congo where it is spoken by all or a large percentage of the nationals.

In Kenya, the Waswahili were, in the beginning, not successful in their attempt to trade with the interior peoples. This lateness in opening up the Kenyan hinterland is often attributed to the Maasai, who, it is claimed, did not easily permit "foreigners" to traverse their territory. On the other hand, there were the Mijikenda and, later, Kamba middlemen who turned out to be as aggressive as the Waswahili in trade. Thirdly, it appears that while the Tanzanian Waswahili had a strong sponsor in the Sultan of Zanzibar, Kenyan Waswahili were not that lucky and had to depend on their own resources. Consequently, their language was not spoken by many people outside its coastal native environment until the 20th Century.

Religion

It is common knowledge that all ethnic Waswahili and Swahilised peoples (except partly-Swahilised former slaves) are Muslims. Islam is the native religion of these people just as it is the native religion of various non-Arab people around the world such as Hausa, Fulani (West Africa), Malay (Malaysia), Turks (Turkey), Indonesians (Indonesia), Pakistanis (Pakistan), Iranians (Iran), etc. It is not Islam, nevertheless, that gets the credit for Kiswahili's phenomenal development in the East and Central African region where the religion was not as successful as in North and West Africa. Ironically, the credit for Kiswahili's good show in the region goes to Christianity, Islam's arch-rival here.

Christian missionaries were the first to reduce Kiswahili grammar into writing; and here, the works of Ludwig Krapf and Bishop Steere are the best references. The United Mission to Central Africa headed by the latter was wholly responsible for the standardisation of this language - a difficult and arbitrary task, given its 15-plus dialects. East Africans today owe their standard form of the language to Dr. Edward Steere and his mission in Zanzibar.

Kenyan missionaries were generally pro-Kiswahili even though some were against it (viewing it as a vehicle of Islam). This was clearly reflected in the views of the Binns and Beecher educational reports of 1940s-50 which blocked the language's development as a medium of instruction because, as it was argued, such development would retard the growth of English and the other African languages (Sifuna, 1989; Wanjala,1985). However, in earlier decades of 20th Century, this fear was not prevalent among missionaries. Mombasa missions, through Rev. John Arthur and the town's

Bishop, passionately pleaded a strong case against English displacing Kiswahili as the lingua franca. The missions used Kiswahili as a language of instruction in classes IV and V (CEEAP, 1919).

In Congo, Rwanda and Burundi, Swedish Missions attempted something like what Dr. Steere had done, namely: to standardise Kiswahili in that sub-region so that it could conform to the East African Standard Kiswahili (Whiteley, 1969). Although the attempt failed to capture the enthusiasm of Kiswahili speakers there, who viewed the dialect as foreign to their locality, the whole effort was not a complete failure as the missionaries' determination appears to have positively influenced the people's attitudes towards the language.

Although Uganda Missions were generally against using Kiswahili for evangelical and other purposes, some individual missionaries were strongly supportive of it. Lumbasio (1990) cites Bishop Willis who was of the opinion that Kiswahili's proper status in Uganda be nothing short of a lingua franca. Another Uganda-based missionary, Father J. Bergman, a Catholic priest, was not only against teaching English at the elementary level of education but openly advocated Kiswahili as the medium of instruction at that level (Lumbasio, 1990). Probably as a result of his campaign, or because of the fact that the Bible had already been translated into Kiswahili in Zanzibar, and not as yet in the local languages of Uganda, instruction in some areas of the country was, to begin with, in this language (Ladefoged, et. al. 1971).

Politics

From the onset, the colonists realised that they needed a "common language" they could use to communicate with their African "subjects". While they probably could have preferred their own languages, language policies that could be required to convert colonial languages into mass languages in the colonies would have required the unequivocal support of the "subjects" themselves, which would have required a lot of energy, vast amounts of resources and great amounts of easily accessible funds, among other things. Language development had to be the number one priority. As this was not easy, rulers in Tanzania (Tanganyika) and the Democratic Republic of Congo, for example, opted for the next sensible option: to choose from among hundreds of African languages one that claimed a majority of speakers without being too controversial.

In Tanzania mainland (then Tanganyika), the Germans had no difficulty in choosing Kiswahili, because it had recorded great success and was satisfactorily widespread. In Congo, the Belgians were daunted by the idea of having to choose from over 200 languages, with four of them: Kiswahili, Lingala, Ki-Kongo and Tchiluba being spoken widely in four different regions of that vast country. The rulers decided that the chosen language must not be a language *d'importation Europeene'* but rather *'une langue veritable*', neither a lingua franca nor a *sabir* (Whiteley, 1969, p. 73). Some circles on the Belgian side strongly supported Kiswahili.

In Kenya and Uganda, however, the situation was quite different. On the one hand, the British rulers imposed their language, while on the other, they appeared to give recognition to a localised language policy (the vernacular theory) in both countries. Yet again in both countries, the policy dictated that the so-called vernaculars should have a very limited, ill-defined role, which could not necessarily undermine English's super-ordinate position. This was more so in Kenya than in Uganda where the role of local languages was less vague. Nonetheless, in both cases, what ensued was a sharp rivalry, not between the local languages and English but among local languages.

The picture we have, at this juncture, is that whoever wielded political power determined the nature of the language policies. He also had all the say as to which language was to influence the people's lives and to what extent; the actual number of its speakers and how wide or narrow its geographical spread notwithstanding. Such was the case during the colonial era as it may to some extent still be the case today.

With independence, however, there has been some evaluation of language policies, particularly in East Africa. Kiswahili is, today, Tanzania's, Kenya's, and even Uganda's national language (at least in theory so far in the latter country). Many a young, highly educated Tanzanian and Kenyan (including people with doctorates from prestigeous Western universities) are opting to write their fiction in their national language.

In regard to this deliberate shift in priority, Roscoe (1977) has given three explanations: (1) "The pernicious effects of English (and the other Western languages) on the broadly egalitarian societies of traditional Africa" (p.4.); (2) Kiswahili's classlessness, its status as a people's language, its lack of identification with "... elitist castes" (Roscoe, 1977, p. 4) and (3) "If a writer sees that there is a growing audience for his works in his own language and finds publishers prepared to produce books for this market, he is likely to find English as his chosen medium suddenly weaker" (Roscoe, 1977, p. 4).

Chapter Six

The Spread of Kiswahili in Eastern and Central Africa

Tanzania

Mother tongue and second language

Kiswahili has recorded its greatest success, so far, in Tanzania. In Zanzibar (including Pemba), even though there are other languages such as Arabic and Hindi/Gujerati, Kiswahili tends to be either the first mother tongue or the second mother tongue of all inhabitants. The autonomous government of the islands, thus, is totally dominated by Kiswahili. It is the national, and official language as well as the language of instruction even though recent trends seem to point to a favouring of bilingualism as the British Council was recently invited by the government to help develop English there.

The situation is not very different in mainland Tanzania because Kiswahili is the national and official language there as well. The only difference is that, off the Coast, the majority of Tanzanians speak the language as a second language. Even so, it could still be regarded as a second mother tongue because most Tanzanians use it in the same way they use their ethnic languages: that is, with parents, immediate relatives, peers and neighbours. It is thus more expedient that when one is analysing the language situation in Tanzania, one talks about ethnic language and national language instead of mother tongue and second language where the latter refers to Kiswahili. In this region, the expression "second language" may be more appropriately used to refer to English and other foreign languages; even other ethnic languages.

Historical development of Kiswahili

Kiswahili is the ethnic language of the Waswahili of Zanzibar and Pemba, the Wahadimu, Watumbatu, Waunguja (Zanzibar) and Wapemba (Pemba island). It would appear that all settlers in these islands were Swahilised in varying degrees. For example, members of the former Sultans' clan, the Busaidis, all from Oman, were Swahilised. Swahilised too, were trading Indians, free Africans who came to Zanzibar and Pemba from the mainland during the last century, and former slaves.

In mainland Tanzania, the aggressive entrepreneurship of the coastal Waswahili and their Arab sponsors initially helped spread Kiswahili among peoples whose mother tongues, even though linguistically related to it, being Bantu, still had certain differences with the language. Then, during the reign of the Germans, Kiswahili was used for official purposes. The Germans appointed Kiswahili-speaking people in junior administrative positions. The junior officers, known as *akidas* and *jumbes*, helped interpret German policies to their fellow Africans who, in most cases, comprehended Kiswahili.

The coming of the British did not offset this equilibrium. While it is true that the British introduced their language and did everything to promote it, they did not try to turn the language clock back by rigorously campaigning or supporting vigorous campaigns against Kiswahili as they did in Kenya and Uganda. Instead, they used the same system of *akidas* and *jumbes* that their predecessors had used before them.

With such a strong Kiswahili foundation, it was quite natural for Tanzanian agitators for independence to adopt the langauge as their tool for their political campaigns. It was the chosen language of TANU (Tanganyika African National Union), the main political party that eventually wrested independence from the British. "Julius K. Nyerere, (Tanu's President), who subsequently became Tanganyika's first Head of State, saw Kiswahili as a medium of national rather than tribal aspirations. A statesman, scholar and poet, he was quick to see the point at which politics, language and literature met" (Roscoe, 1977, p. 3).

Support for Kiswahili

Kiswahili's supporters have been more coherent in Tanzania than in any other country in the region. They have showered Kiswahili with the fullest of praises while being very careful to explain quite clearly what its merits and demerits are, not failing, at the same time, to say how the latter are to be overcome. As perhaps expected, President Nyerere went ahead to declare Kiswahili the national and official language of Tanganyika soon after independence. In Zanzibar, President Karume (later, also the first Vice-President of the Union of Tanzania) had no big choice to make. In his country, there had been no history of language rivalry. Besides, "he had no command of English at all" (Roscoe, 1977, p. 4).

Nyerere's vision, even though fundamental, only matched but did not surpass that of other supporters of Kiswahili in Tanzania, some of whom began agitating for the language long before the president-to-be began pressing for independence. Note that Shaaban Robert, the legendary East African Kiswahili poet and novelist from (former) Tanganyika was already extolling the language's virtues and agitating for its use in education, an idea that Nyerere, the politician, would help partially realise two decades later. In one of his poems, published in a book entitled *Pambo La Lugha*, Shaaban Robert says:

> Swahili is rich, in its elegance and proverbs, and I think
> *in the near future, it will be possible to translate many*

fields of education (italics added) and render a service to mankind both with insight and beauty, mother's breast is sweet, no other satisfies (cited in Whiteley, 1969, p. 136).

After independence, Kiswahili gained more supporters and promoters who became bolder and more assertive. One promoter, S. Mushi, appraised the language's role in the first half of the 1960s thus:

> The role played by Swahili language in Tanzania is immense. Almost everybody in Tanzania can speak the language: and, therefore, it has become a useful medium of communication. Since the language has now become the national language, we feel we must do something to widen its scope so that it may be sufficiently useful in all Government activities, in schools and commercial circles. We want to rid the language of bad influences and to guide it to grow along the proper road. We want to standardise (sic) its orthography and usage, and to encourage all our people to learn to speak and write properly grammatical Swahili (cited in Whiteley, 1969, p. 104).

This positive attitude to Kiswahili finds an echo in official utterances of that time. Whiteley (1969) informs us that late in 1964, the Second Vice President of Tanzania sent a circular to civil servants and others urging them to desist from the habit of mixing Swahili and English (p. 105). The Second Vice President also assertively referred

> to a time when "kazi zetu zote na za kila namna zitaendeshwa kwa Kiswahili" (all our work will be conducted with use of the Kiswahili medium) and a second statement, of 4 January 1967 has directed that Swahili be used for all Government business, and that the use of English or any other foreign languages unnecessarily is to cease forthwith. All ministries, district councils, co-operative unions, and parastatal organisations are therefore obliged to use Swahili in their day-to-day business". (Cited in Whiteley, 1969, p. 137).

Why Kiswahili was chosen

Some of the reasons why Kiswahili was chosen as the national/official language of Tanzania, which include its trade links before colonisation, have already been discussed above. These delineate Kiswahili's strengths. Other reasons, however underscore the weaknesses of its main adversary, English. Roscoe (1977) attributes English's contradiction as a language that has developed through its native speaker's history of adventure, war, class stratifications and plunder on the one hand, and Kiswahili's relative lack of a similar history, as having constituted to the latter's choice. He explains this as follows:

> Swahili's adoption as a national language alongside English has important implications for social cohesion. The subtle involvement of language with class involvement, division, and exploitation, is a story sociolinguists are only beginning to relate. Britain introduced into her colonies a language born of a class-ridden society, bearing in its sounds and structure a history of social discrimination, oligarchic gamesmanship, and inhumanity .
>
> What seems clear about Kiswahili, .i.Tanzania:creative writers;however, especially in Tanzania, is its classlessness, its status as a people's language, its lack of identification with Mandarin groups and elitist castes. This is important, for it means that where once only a small pool of English-speakers was available for posts in government and administration (and these not necessarily representing the nation's best minds and abilities), an imaginative language policy now allows Tanzania to recruit widely among its people. It is significant ... that the late Second Vice-President, Abeid .i.Karume, Abeid;Karume, had no command of English at all (Roscoe, 1977, p. 4).

Creative writing

Very few Tanzanians are known to have written their works of fiction in English. However, writers like Gabriel Ruhumbika, the writer of *Village in Uhuru*, Peter Palangyo who wrote *Dying in the Sun*, Ismael R. Mbise: *Blood on Our*

Land, W.E. Mkufya: *The Wicked Walk,* and Hamza Sokko: *The Gathering Storm* have published work in English.

These five and their likes cannot be said to represent Tanzanian writers, however, for they have not been known to be popular. Popular writing in Tanzania has been, since colonial days and possibly prior to that, in Kiswahili. Some of the creative artists beginning with the country's best known writer, Shaaban Robert, who wrote his novels and poems from the first half of the 1940s to the late 1950s, may turn out to have written up some of the best East African literature, most of it in Kiswahili.

This tradition of writing in Kiswahili certainly did not, and apparently will not end with Shaaban Robert; as other established writers today have followed his footsteps. About this turn of events, Roscoe (1977) has said:

> Several young East African writers (are) already producing work in both Swahili and English. Furthermore, the number of writers who want to work only in the local language has increased sharply since the status of Swahili was officially recognised by the post-colonial language policies of all East African territories. The position of English is no longer as secure as it was (p. 4).

The true worth of this statement may be more easily observed in Tanzania than in any of the other East African territories. It is in Tanzania where doctorate holders such as Euphrase Kezilahabi, the novelist and Ebrahim Hussein, the playwright have produced some of the best East African literary works — all in Kiswahili. Novels of a high calibre have also been written by the Zanzibari writer, Said Ahmed Mohamed, while serious plays have been written by arguably one of the most accomplished female writers in Africa, Penina Muhando.

All these writers are college-educated and adequately tutored in English in both local and foreign universities. S.A. Mohamed, for example, has a doctorate from

Germany while Professor Muhando Mlama is a graduate of the University of Dar es Salaam. Their choice of Kiswahili as a literary medium is therefore not a mere coincidence but a deliberate move in favour of writing in the language - an African language, their language.

Language of "pop"

Whereas the political implications of Kiswahili's advancement in Tanzania may not be fully appreciated across the region, as the nationals of neighbouring countries may have cause to feel jealous and, thus, intentionally resist being drawn into a race whose results are easily predictable, the youth in the sister states have never been able or even willing to resist the sweet melodies of Kiswahili music from among the best composers in the region. In other words, Kiswahili music from Tanzania has had a pervasive influence on generations of music lovers in East and Central Africa just as English music from America is threatening to conquer the world.

It all began with the Rumba/Pachanga/Kirikiri/ Soukous revolution in Congo Kinshasa/Congo Brazaville from the late 1940s; a revolution inspired by familiar melodies from the Caribbean/Latin American region which had, in turn, been inspired by ancient African rhythms through the creativity of African slaves and freed slaves in the Western hemisphere. Then, some time in the 1950s, Tanzanians began to copy the rhythms from the Congos; but while Congolese sang mainly in Lingala, Tanzanians opted to sing in Kiswahili. With time, young musically talented Tanzanians mastered the rhythms and no longer had to copy Congolese compositions. From then on, great music from Tanzania began to dominate the East African scene. Thereby, Kiswahili gained another boost — music — whose power over the senses is a common knowlege vehicle.

To the extent that, while at school young people read Shaaban Robert's Kiswahili novels and recited his poetry, at home (with the aid of the cheap transitor radio) and in social halls and bars, they and/or their elders listened to the throbbing drums of Atomic Jazz Band, Morogoro Jazz, Jamhuri Jazz, Western Jazz, Kilwa Jazz, Vijana Jazz, Safari Trippers, Tabora Jazz. Later, Milimani Park Jazz, Orchestre Juata Jazz, Afro 70, and many others joined the arena. The latter band was the most successful as a group in Africa in the 1970s as, during the Second Back and African Cultural Festival held at Lagos in 1977, it distinguished itself by coming second only to Stevie Wonder (U.S.A.) and, consequently, flooring such internationally renowned single stars and groups as Miriam Makeba and the British-based Ghanian group Osibisa. Makeba and Osibisa came third and fourth respectively.

The young and old music lovers listened to or danced to the rhythms of their favourite music, being endeared to Kiswahili through the media. And as the musicians perfected their art, in no time, a lot of music lovers were singing quietly to themselves the great compositions of musicians who had attained prominence. Such musicians as John Kijiko, Wema Abdallah, Juma Kilaza, Ahmed Kipande, Duncan Njilima, Patrick Balisidya, Wilson Peter Kinyonga, "Chiriku" Hemedi Maneti, George Peter Kinyonga and the greatest of all time (the Tanzanian musicians that influenced East Africans most): Salum Abdallah (Cuban Marimba Jazz) and Mbarak Mwineshehe Mwaruka (Morogoro Jazz/Orchestre-Super Volcano) all thrilled the music lovers.

It has been said that literature reflects the culture of the writer(s) and has either a positive or negative influence on the readers. But music affects one more because it claims the most pervasive effect on its audience as it invades the listener from all soft points, overwhelming him or her with the greatest urgency, appealing to his experiences of himself/herself and his/her immediate as well as wider environment. It is in this way that Michael Jackson is said to be recording the greatest success in a bid to conquer the U.S.S.R. and China on behalf of America where the seemingly all-powerful politico-military vehicle of Pentagon/Nato/Kennedy/Nixon/Carter/Reagan/Bush has made very little advance over the ages. Whereas young Russians and their Chinese peers will madly dance and/or sentimentally listen to Michael Jackson's songs, they will not similarly dance to the tune of the American political proselytising. Not thoughtlessly, in any event.

It is in this manner that Tanzanian musicians have succeeded in winning the hearts of many East Africans, scoring a great many points for Kiswahili in the process. Thus, one may want to view Michael Jackson as America's best cultural and linguistic ambassador (the English language has gained a great deal from Michael Jackson's music bomb just as German was boosted by Beethoven's excellent compositions). Similarly, one may put Mbarak Mwinshehe Mwaruka and Salum Abdallah (among others) in the same slot, in this region.

Kenya

Approach-avoidance conflict

Whereas Tanzania has been characterised by a realistic approach to Kiswahili, Kenya has been suffering from what psychologists call the approach-avoidance conflict; a conflict that has slowed the development of the language in this country. Consequently, Kenya is still in the process of getting out of this situation, an unfortunate situation decried by the country's leading Kiswahili scholars. The late Jay Kitsao of the University of Nairobi, had this to say:

> Swahili as Kenya's national language is not making the expected progress due to a combination of factors including two important ones. First, the layman at the bottom and the fruits-of-Uhuru-eating boss in the office

do not know, nor do they care to learn the language, since there is really not the need to do so. Second, the elite consider themselves apart from Kiswahili or worse, their mother tongue. Clearly therefore, if we are to realise the full benefits of having Kiswahili as a tool of a national communication, a lot still remains to be done... a pathetic case because, although Kiswahili started in Kenya, efforts to develop it have been left to Tanzania alone (cited in Lumbasio, 1990, p. 31).

Kitsao is supported, in view of the lackadaisical commitment by Kenyan officials as well as intellectuals to Kiswahili, by Ireri Mbaabu of Kenyatta University. Mbaabu not only describes Kenyans' lack of commitment to their declared national language but goes farther to appeal to their emotions by reminding them that, even though, historically, Kiswahili's native land is Kenya, it is Tanzania that is taking all the credit by her manifest enthusiasm in developing it. Kenya is, thereby, decidedly being outpaced by Tanzania. According to him, Kenya has a maternal duty to win the medal. Says Mbaabu:

> Kiswahili started on the Kenyan Coast. The spread was southwards from Kenya to Tanzania. We cannot afford to stand aside and wait for Tanzania to give us all the innovations, technical terms and other aspects of internal language planning as we currently seem to be doing. We should lend a hand in moulding this fast developing language for our national goals. As the mother, Kenya should not be satisfied in watching her offspring fostered by a step-mother while she is in a better position of upbringing her child - Kiswahili (cited in Lumbasio, 1990, p.32).

Language policies and linguistic distribution

The reasons that resulted in this attitude to Kiswahili in Kenya, which has been at best sluggish and at worst lukewarm if not outrightly hostile, are many, but three may be cited here. The glaring one is, viewed cursorily, the colonial approach to African languages in Kenya. Underlying this is the attitude of the colonists towards African languages (and aything African generally) in a country that they once baptised and fondly referred to as "The White Man's Country". Unlike Tanzania and Uganda, Kenya was, after colonialism entrenched itself, never meant to be an independent African country. Like Zimbabwe and South Africa, Kenya was a white man's country. The country had, therefore, to evolve a unique European character. This character was, needless to say, opposed to all African norms and values. Being an African language, Kiswahili, quite naturally, was a target for suppression.

The other reason was a consequence of the first. Two lateral movements in colonial Kenya led to a further degradation of Kiswahili. One was the upgrading of English as the 'civilised language' (the language of the elites and the well-to-do). In no time, Africans not only looked up to English as the key to "progress", but also as a language that was inherently and infinitely superior to their own languages whose "flaws" became more and more obvious to them in every way. Needless to say, the weaknesses of African languages only became more obvious to the Africans as colonialist propagandists either covertly suggested the existence of such flaws; or when this civilised approach did not seem to work, openly pointed them out, taking care to graphically describe how, for example, these languages lacked sufficient vocabulary for academic purposes. Ingeniously fabricated detail was within easy access to propagandists.[101]

As the battle to equate English with civilisation raged on and was being won by its determined native speakers, a parallel downward movement to relate African languages (Kiswahili among them) and Africans themselves with primitivity (the opposite of civilisation) was also being won by the same British colonists. Viewed from both angles, the Africans were losing.

Then an unfortunate thing happened. The African reacted by running away from anything "savage" ... his culture, language and even himself. Africans wanted to be associated with civilisation, and thus in no time, they started echoing all the lies of the colonialists with regard to African cultures, languages and people. The admittance that Kiswahili was inferior to English, in a way reflected this. In other words, Kenyan Africans had come to accept that they needed English, among other wonderful things the British had in store, "to civilise them".

The third reason was the composition of the African socio-political-linguistic groupings or, in other words, the ethnic groups, the so-called "tribes". With a great amount of fanning from the same colonial propagandists, the Bantu/non-Bantu divide was felt more sharply in Kenya than in Uganda (where the divide should have been more acute) or Tanzania (where the factor was, apparently, non-existent). In Kenya, non-Bantus, especially the Luo, felt that any language policy that would favour the adoption of Kiswahili to any elevated status would put them at a disadvantage vis-a-vis the majority Bantu groups since Kiswahili was a Bantu language (Whiteley, 1969). Ironically, the Luos did not find anything wrong with accepting English, which was not even an African language! To cap it all, Luos have produced some of the most articulate orators in the English language in Kenya if not in the whole of Africa. The memorable native-like rhetoric of individuals such as the late Tom Mboya and the late Robert Ouko, among others, is not easily matched by second language speakers anywhere.

The language of political parties during the colonial era

Whiteley (1969) reports that "KANU (Kenya African National Union), the national unity party that eventually won Kenya's independence from the British, started off by advocating Kiswahili as the language for the whole country and produced their party paper in it. Later, however, perhaps in deference to their party membership, they favoured the three main local languages, Kikuyu, Kamba, and Luo"(p. 68).

It is not clear what Whiteley means by "in deference to their party membership"; but, just in case he meant the ethnic composition of the membership of the party, then KADU (Kenya African Democratic Union) should have been in more trouble since it embraced a multitude of small socio-politico-linguistic groupings with a myriad of languages and dialects (more often than not viewed as separate languages). Instead, "KADU... by contrast... increasingly favoured the use of Swahili" (Whiteley, 1969, p. 68). Whiteley (1969) intimates that the very ethnic composition of KADU, affiliation to the smaller tribal units (p. 68) may have been responsible for the party's unwavering support for Kiswahili since its members could have found it a difficult task indeed to choose from the multiplicity of their languages and dialects. This argument has some weight, but then only in the context of the Kenya of those days. Otherwise if one were to make a comparison with the situation in Tanganyika in those days, the argument at once loses its weight. For Tanganyika not only had many more smaller "tribes", she also had mega-tribes such as the Chagga, Nyakusya, Sukuma and Ha, which were, individually, bigger than any big "tribe" in Kenya.

The real reason why KANU started with Kiswahili and then switched to ethnic languages is because of the political and language backgrounds from which both KANU and KADU were founded. One needs to study the language policies in Kenya against the socio-political situation, then compare them to manifestations of the same factors in any one of her neighbouring sister states. It will be observed, for example, that, whereas Tanzanians came to independence almost intact, less dehumanised, more confident of themselves as a people equal to anybody, anywhere, and above all, unified to a greater degree, Kenyans arrived at the same venue greatly debased, their confidence in everything tarnished, to a great extent feeling inferior to white people and white things, and extremely divided. It is no wonder that the language policies of these two parties were "vigorous but by no means consistent" (Whiteley, 1969, p. 68). Whiteley (1969), therefore, hits the nail right on the head when he describes this situation as "typical of the ambivalent attitude that has characterised all language policies in Kenya" (p. 68). Only Whiteley's is an understatement. He would have summed it all quite satisfactorily had he observed ambivalence in almost anything of note in Kenya including the African's attitude towards any black person and everything related to that person.

Such is the situation described as approach-avoidance conflict earlier on in this section. It is this conflict that plagued Kenyans during the colonial era; and the hangover still pervades the atmosphere to this day.

As it was then, the two parties could not underestimate the significance of Kiswahili among the Kenyan electorate, even with Kanu's "minor" defection. "Swahili was, of course, of crucial importance to both parties, whatever their avowed policy" (Whiteley, 1969, p. 68). So it is now, that even though Kiswahili is Kenya's national language and, as such, no party can defect from that line, the attitude towards the language among the "Western educated", a good number of whom may view themselves as more civilised than the uneducated "illiterates," remains much the same as it was during the colonial days. To this clique, Kiswahili is the language of the "servants"; that is, the riffraff of the society. (Note that during the colonial era, only black-skinned people were servants to the lighter skinned in the main, and the language between the masters and servants was *ki-Setla,* the Europeans' pidgin Kiswahili.) The elites avoid the language as such, but they use it to relate cross-ethnically when they do not want to sound "too official" or "too European" by using English, a language that will just not be nativised in Kenya, and has thus adamantly remained foreign-sounding. They also use Kiswahili to appeal to a sense of brotherliness and/or comradeship. More significantly, they use it to rally support from a linguistically diversified electorate, and also in times of confrontation with elites from neighbouring countries, or whenever there is a national crisis.

The situation above describes the older generation of elites. With younger Kenyans, however, the situation is noticeably different. Those who were very young when Kenya regained her independence, or were not yet born, manifest a more positive attitude towards their national language. One reason why this is so could be because many are uprooted from their ancestral "homelands" at a very tender age responding to the dictates of modern living and preoccupations which require them to seek boarding schools and jobs outside their so-called "home-areas". While away from "home" the young people come across many people who do not necessarily speak their mother tongues and are forced by circumstances to interact with them. Throughout their lives, these "uprooted peoples" often speak their native tongues less frequently than they speak Kiswahili.

The question of alternative "national" languages

It has been severally suggested that one reason why Kiswahili's development in independent Kenya was slowed is that the Luo ethnic group, one of pre-independence Kanu's ethnic pillars, was not in favour of the language because Luos did not want to be swamped-in. Since they were non-Bantu, and Kiswahili is a Bantu language, they stood at a great disadvantage in accepting it. A number of Luos who were quite influential, thus did their best to block Kiswahili's upgrading to national language status. Others went as far as suggesting Dholuo, their ethnic language, to be considered as the alternative to Kiswahili in the position of the all-national language. These people pointed out Dholuo's merits viewed from the angle of Kiswahili's demerits.

Ironically, Bantu, Kikuyu and Kamba were, at the same time, also doing their best, not to further the advancement of Kiswahili because it is Bantu, but to block its advancement, arguing that it was no more national than Gikuyu, Kikamba, Dholuo or any other Kenyan national language for that matter. Some denigrated its Arabic influences as evidence of its not being fully African let alone Bantu. There were those who viewed Kiswahili as purely Arabic.

The debate intensified with indications that the government was about to announce a major language policy in the late 1960s and early 1970's. This debate was only checked in its tracks (though not without great grumbling), in 1974 when the then President, Mr. Jomo Kenyatta, endorsed the 1969 Kanu Governing Council decision that Kiswahili be the officially recognised national language of independent Kenya. He, at the same time, suggested that all parliamentary debates be conducted in the national language. Nevertheless, the Kiswahili national language debate was only checked but not entirely put to an end.

The state of affairs that bred all the jockeying for the all-national position on behalf of the other ethnic languages rather than Kiswahili amazed and riled Kenyan linguists and those others with some knowledge of linguistics, who knew perfectly well that Kiswahili was no more Arabic than any other Kenyan "national" language. They could not see the rationale in trying to block Kiswahili on grounds that there were other languages that qualified more as national languages than Kiswahili.

One of the foremost critics of promoters of ethnic languages at the expense of Kiswahili was Chris Wanjala, a Kenyan professor of literature who is cited by

Lumbasio (1990) as putting forward the following arguments:-

1. A nation needs to have a national language.
2. Kiswahili is that declared national language in Kenya.
3. Writers ought to strive to reach the rural population with writing in the national language.
4. Kenyans should strive to be proficient in Kiswahili.
5. They should stop wrangling about the language that better qualifies as the national language even after years of Kiswahili as the declared national language.
6. That some African countries that do not have a popular all-national language such as those of West Africa envy Kenyans about their language.
7. That while Kenyans are taking too long to recognise their national language and accept it as an assct instead of viewing it as a liability, people from all over the world were streaming into East Africa to learn this language. The situation in Kenya is unfortunate because Kenyans themselves do not bother to study it and enhance its growth.

The Luo, non-Bantu factor revisited

The contention that Luos are bound to face some disadvantages in learning Kiswahili as compared to members of the Bantu groups may amount to a gross exaggeration. This is so particularly when the issue is viewed against the ability of some members of this socio-politico-linguistic group to acquire English so impressively, even to a state of perfection. One thus needs not search far for the real cause of rejection of Kiswahili by Luos. As with other groups that tried to block the decision to make Kiswahili Kenya's de jure national language, one finds a political motive to Luos' approach-avoidance conflict with Kiswahili, which may be traced back to the divide-and-rule tactics employed by British colonists in Kenya.

Kenyans were deliberately pitted against other Kenyans. On one side were ranged the Luo-Kikuyu-Kamba power blocks. On the other side were various pockets of the small tribes not only from the Bantu cluster but also from the Nilotic, Nilo-Cushitic and Cushitic clusters! Thus, while the Luos were protesting Bantu, most Kalenjin, Turkana, Rendille, Maasai, Somali, all non-Bantu, were in KADU, and not only advocating for, but actually using Kiswahili in party and other matters..! Repeat: *They are all non-Bantu.* Furthermore, Luos in Tanzania never protested Bantu. Today, Luos in that country are as proficient in Kiswahili as any other Tanzanians, Bantu or non-Bantu. The same can be said about some Luos even in Kenya as Roscoe (1977) shows.

One thus can never find credence in the linguistic reasoning against Kiswahili. Such reasoning tapers off when one takes even the most casual glance at the political alliances that produced the heated politicking of the late 50's and early 60's.

The situation in Uganda is quite the opposite. The Bantu-speaking groups rejected Kiswahili while the Nilotes (Luos are Nilotes) embraced it with open arms! This would mean that even the Luos in Uganda supported the use of Kiswahili. Whiteley (1969) summarises this state of affairs in the following manner:

> It is interesting to note the support for Swahili among the Nilotes in Uganda, in contrast to the opposition from them in Kenya, which does something to dispel the myth that there are linguistic reasons why Nilotes find Swahili difficult to learn. In Uganda, where the Nilotes were weak in relation to the lake kingdoms, notably the Ganda, Swahili was both a unifying influence and a means of buttressing their position by stressing the links with Swahili speakers elsewhere. In Kenya, where the Luo were a relatively powerful group, Swahili served to diminish their position by merging

them with the rest of the Bantu-speaking groups of the country (p. 71).

What is more interesting is the way Luos in the three countries (Kenya, Tanzania and Uganda) reacted to Kiswahili with the advent of independence. It is surprising to see how differently members of one ethnic group behaved towards the language. The evidence we have, clearly shows that the kind of politics each country practised influenced this ethnic group's reaction. Tanzania, which devalued tribal influence of its politics, did not have to worry about possible resistance to its language policies from any of its 120-plus ethnic groups. Significantly the Luo factor, or any other tribal factors, did not feature here. Uganda, whose kingdoms were tribe-based, and where Luos did not belong to any of the kingdoms, they (Luos) actually embraced Kiswahili. To them, Kiswahili was a handy weapon against domination by the kingdoms. Kenya necessarily had the Luo factor because tribal allegiances were very instrumental in Kenyan politics.

Developing the national language

The question of how to go about developing the national language has never been coherently addressed at the national level in Kenya. From the top echelons of government circles down to the ordinary citizen in the countryside, nobody seems to be able to articulate what Kiswahili's true status really is; and the outcome has been that no one has felt any obligation to give the language any due consideration let alone respect. The notion most Kenyans have is that Kiswahili is not very important, or to be more precise, it is a language *that will take nobody anywhere.*

This attitude was clearly reflected in a statement made by the once powerful first Attorney General of independent Kenya, who later became the Minister for Constitutional Affairs, Mr. Charles M. Njonjo. In the 1970s, right after Kiswahili had been declared the country's national language, Njonjo said that he did not understand all the fuss over the much attention given to the language in school as anybody could pick it from the streets(!). This message was carried in all the daily newspapers, and it may have reinforced the already vague approach to the whole question by the citizenry at large, which had been tutored over the years to view English and English only as the key language to all imaginable as well as unimaginable progress! As a point of emphasis, it will be noted that Mr. Njonjo did not, in the same vein, suggest that English ought to receive less attention than what it was receiving, which was overwhelming, even in spite of the fact that it was Kiswahili that was the national language.

On the whole, then, suggestions as to how the language ought to be developed have come from individuals whose power to influence national decisions is minimal indeed. One of such individuals is Mohammed Bakari, then a senior lecturer in Linguistics at the University of Nairobi and now a professor in Islamic studies there. He said:

> Kiswahili must be taught in Kenya's schools if the national culture has to be promoted; graduates who are well equipped in Linguistics and Kiswahili Literature and grammar should be fully utilised in translating the folklore of their various ethnic backgrounds into Kiswahili so as to enrich the national language and culture....
>
> Kiswahili literature should be taken as the matrix on which the regional oral traditions should eventually be incorporated into the national literature that would reflect the value systems of the larger Kenyan culture. Oral traditions should be collected, documented and translated into Swahili and either poeticised or fictionalised in creative writings (cited in Lumbasio, 1990, p. 19).

E.N. Wanyoike (cited in Lumbasio, 1990) and Petronilla Lumbasio hold a similar view to Bakari's. They both feel that there is a need to teach Kiswahili in

Kenya as apposed to "picking it from the streets". Wanyoike's argument is that the English, the Germans and the French teach their children their mother tongues. It is more needful therefore for Kenyans also to teach their own children Kiswahili which is the mother tongue of very few schoolgoers in Kenya. Lumbasio stresses this point further by pointing out that for most Kenyans, Kiswahili is a second language and thus their first languages are likely to interfere with their Kiswahili. She intimates that the way out of a possible flooding of many Kiswahilis in one country is to teach the standard form thoroughly (Lumbasio, 1990).

One never easily finds such clarity of intent in official and educational circles. What Kenyans are used to are policies without corresponding concrete planning or even coherent descriptions of language development plans.

Landmarks for Kiswahili's advancement

In Kenya, the survival of Kiswahili as the topmost language has been so threatened that government policies have always come as critical surprises. Furthermore, rarely have such policies been followed by observable implementation; to the extent that detractors have had the nerve to challenge their legitimacy and efficacy, not once but quite often. Apparently, the message that has been trickling down to the detractors is that such policies, not followed by action, are not decisive and are thus open to criticism.

As people get persuaded to accept the fact that there are not two, three or just any number of national languages in Kenya, but just one: (Kiswahili) and that the situation is irreversible, there remains no option but to see the advantages of having one common medium of communication countrywide, that is, one local language. After all is said and done, Kenyans come to realise that the decision to make Kiswahili a national language was, after all, one of the wisest made in independent Kenya.

The Presidents' stand

Kiswahili owes its rise from uncertainty to its precariously secure position today in this country to two major announcements made at an interval of about a decade by two Presidents: Kenyatta (the first) and Moi (the second). The first landmark was when President Kenyatta, acting on the 1969 Kanu Governing Council decision, announced that Kiswahili had changed its status from a *de facto* to the *de jure* national language of Kenya, in 1974. The second landmark is when President Moi, acting on the recommendation of the Mackay Education Commission he had appointed, directed that Kiswahili be examined at the primary school level and be a compulsory examinable subject at the high school level. Not until then did foot-dragging Kenyans begin to take the language seriously, as it could now lead somebody somewhere.

These landmarks encouraged Kiswahili enthusiasts in Kenya a great deal. Some are already anticipating the third landmark: when Kiswahili will be made the language of instruction.

Kiswahili in education

While politicians have been mainly politicking without giving concrete direction on the development of Kiswahili, educationists have been openly less enthusiastic about government euphoria with regard to the language. From the very beginning, educationists have come to be associated with equivocation whenever the question of Kiswahili has surfaced.

Consider the following statement by Professor Ominde, head of the first education commission in independent Kenya:

> Kiswahili is the principal common medium of East Africa and beyond. We agree with the overwhelming majority of our witnesses in desiring to see Kiswahili established as a national language in Kenya and we recommend that it should be made a compulsory subject of study in the secondary school (Ominde, 1964, p. 83).

But then he and the other commissioners went ahead and disregarded the language and all other African languages as media of instruction at all levels claiming that the languages were not suited for the task; that only English could be suitable; to wit, they were inferior and English was superior. This pioneering Kenya Education Commission did nothing to deal decisively with the great imbalance between Kiswahili and English in regard to the number of periods allotted to each subject a week in schools. The fact that English had the lion's share of allotment on the school timetables did not bother the commissioners. The favoured language (English) enjoyed eight hours a week whereas the national language had only three at the primary school level. No position was defined for the language at the secondary school level by the Minister of Education. What this meant was that Kiswahili was not going to depend much on the school system in order to become the respected national language.

That was 1964. Thereafter, a whole decade elapsed before Kiswahili could be declared the national language; and at a time when most Kenyans were still reeling from the dehumanising effects of the trauma of colonialism. With the passage of time, it was expected that the things and attitudes that had made Kenyans not value their own worth would change. This was not to be easily so, however.

In 1976, another commission under the chairmanship of the then Permanent Secretary of Education, Mr. Gachathi, issued another vague statement with regard to Kiswahili:

> Kiswahili is one of the languages found in Kenya. Moreover, it is a national language. So it has to be recognised as an important language in education. The government should therefore assist in fostering the development of Kiswahili at both levels (Gachathi, 1976, p.90).

Thus, it is only the (1984) Mackay Commission that had a coherent educational agenda for Kiswahili as a language in education. With the Mackay Commission, there was some observable follow-up action educationally, mentioned earlier on; to wit, the declaration that it be examined at the primary level and, at the same time, making it a compulsory subject at the secondary school level. The action that followed these declarations is what is rapidly changing the attitude of Kenyans, particularly the youths who are the main players, towards the language.

Writing in Kiswahili

Kenyans have been rather slow in deciding to write in Kiswahili. However, the first literary works in Kenya written in Kiswahili can be traced back to the 1950s. Among such works are those of Henry Kuria, *Nakupenda Lakini*, Gerishon Ngugi, *Nimelogwa Nisiwe na Mpenzi*, Kimani wa Nyoike, *Maisha ni Nini*, Leo Odero Omolo, *Mwerevu Hajinyoi*, Kareithi, *Kaburi Bila Msalaba*, and even some by white Kenyans such as Graham Hyslop, who wrote the memorable *Mgeni Karibu* and *Afadhali Mchawi*. Most of these works were written before independence. Kenyans then wrote in Kiswahili regardless of their ethnic backgrounds. Among the writers cited above, are Agikuyu, Luo and English.

The big change came with the emergence of Ngugi wa Thiong'o as a Kenyan writer in the English language. Ngugi's successful writing in the prestigeous language seems to have won the hearts of many Kenyans. Younger people with some talent started to write in the language. Soon, names such as Grace Ogot, Francis Imbuga,

Leonard Kibera, Billy Wandera, Rebecca Njau, Meja Mwangi, Micere Mugo, David Mulwa, Mwangi Ruheni, Thomas Okare and the populist writers, David Maillu and Charles Mangua were on everybody's lips.

The second *big change* came with a sort of 'going back to the basics' phenomenon. Suddenly, highly educated linguists were opting to write in Kiswahili. This movement produced prolific playwrights in the persons of Jay Kitsao, who has a doctorate degree from Nairobi University, and Chacha Nyaigotti Chacha, who holds a doctorate from Yale University in the U.S.A. The same movement also produced one of the finest plays in Kenya if not East Africa, *Kilio cha Haki,* by Al-Amin Mazrui, a Stanford University (U.S.A.) doctorate holder. Mazrui also wrote a collection of controversial poems in Kiswahili *(Chembe cha Moyo)* in the tradition of the new Kiswahili poetry of Ebrahim Hussein *(Ngoma na Vailini)*; Mulokozi and Kahigi *(Malenga wa Bara);* Euphrase Kezilahabi *(Kichomi)* and Said Ahmed Mohammed *(Sikate Tamaa).* The works of these artists threaten to turn the world of Kiswahili poetic tradition upside down. Note that all these writers are holders of Ph.D. mostly from foreign universities.

Nevertheless, classical Kiswahili poetry, which boasts a centuries-old tradition in Kenya, still enjoys most sway among the old and even the young ethnic Waswahili as well as non-ethnic Waswahili who happen to be Kiswahili literature enthusiasts. The recent works of Ahmad Nassir Juma Bhalo: *Malenga wa Mvita,* Abdilatif Abdallah: *Sauti ya Dhiki* and Bukheit Amana: *Malenga wa Vumba,* stand out as literary masterpieces with very few equals in Africa. They are not only excellent in form but also in theme, metaphor, symbolism, imagery and idiom. Ahmad Nassir, Abdilatif, and Bukheit may claim, with a lot of justification, to have properly fitted in the giant footsteps of Kenya's grand poets of all times, Muyaka wa Muhaji of Mombasa (18th-

19th Centuries), and Fumo Liyongo of Pate (8/9th Century).

The Kenyan Kiswahili novel also received a major boost from George Katama Mkangi who, apart from writing his experimental *Ukiwa*, a less successful work in the novel form, later published one of the most sophisticated novels in Kenya today (in Kiswahili), namely: *Mafuta*. He has ever since published an even more sophisticated novel *Walenisi*. These works compare well with some of the best novels by Africans in English and French to date. As with most of the other current writers in Kiswahili in Kenya and East Africa at large, Mkangi has a doctorate from the University of Sussex in England. [117]

And the list is not exhausted. There is for example, Rocha Chimerah's *Nyongo Mkalia Ini*, which easily fits in this category.

The *third great change* was, once again, kicked off by Ngugi wa Thiong'o who, in the late 1970s, decided to write in Gikuyu, his mother tongue, instead of English. As Ngugi has made a great impact not only in Kenya and Africa but the (literary) world-over (two of his works; *A Grain of Wheat* and *Petals of Blood* have become classics), his change of literary medium has sent ripples across the literary world, and influenced young aspiring writers in the country. Quite a number of talented and quasi-talented youths have already experimented with their mother tongues in writing fiction. Even old guards such as Grace Ogot have also joined the new movement. Ogot has already published two short stories in her native Dholuo.

Whether this third change will derail enthusiasm in writing in the national language or not can only be subject to speculation. What seems to constitute a fact, however, is that the Kiswahili current is very strong and may not necessarily clash with the ethnic current. It may, in fact, be the bigger portion of it. This view appears to be shared by the late Professor Whiteley and Professor Ali Mazrui (Roscoe, 1977) to whom the following observation is ascribed:

> (Kiswahili) has dramatically penetrated inland areas and, crucially, has crossed ethnic boundaries; for while it is opposed politically by the Nilotic Luo as being a Bantu language, it is in fact spoken widely by the Luo themselves, and a knowledge of Swahili is universal among their leaders, whether in business, politics or scholarship. *Jared Angira, one of the finest Luo poets, already uses Swahili as well as English* (Italics added) (p. 3).

Another Kenyan writer who has turned his back on English and chosen to write in Kiswahili is David Mulwa, one of the most dedicated Kenyans in theatre, alongside the likes of Tirus Gathwe. Mulwa has written quite a number of plays, such as the memorable *Ukame* and *Buriani* co-authored with Yahya, all in Kiswahili. In fact the writer's only work in English to date is his less successful novel *Master and Servant* and the better celebrated *Redemption*, a play.

Thus, we return right where we begun: Approach-avoidance conflict. Indecision. Confoundment. This is what characterises Kenyan writers' decision on choice of literary medium. This is characteristic of Kenya as a whole, historically.

The situation is nevertheless not totally hopeless, as more and more Kenyans are shedding the misguided notion of English as the honey-coated, prestigious language and are, of their own volition, opting for Kiswahili cross-ethnically as the evidence above suggests. One may surmise that Professor Ali Mazrui's prognostication that Swahili will eventually complete its conquest of (recalcitrant) Kenya (cited in Roscoe, 1977, p.3) is no longer an illusion but a reality.

The language of "pop"

As we said earlier, in Kenya, the situation differs a great deal from that of Tanzania. While it is true that there was such a time when in Kenya, Kiswahili was the language of pop (Whiteley,1969), a time when Tanzanians were still slumbering, musically speaking, that cannot definitely be said to be the case now.

There was that time when, influenced by African-American Jazz and "Twist" beats, which, meshed with African rhythms, talented Kenyans from the late 1940s to early 1960s composed some of the most consummate pieces of music ever in these regions.

This is the time when young music lovers in Nairobi swooned to Daudi Kabaka's strumming of the guitar. They, at the same time, read his lips as he satirised the strange imitative behaviour of Nairobians in particular and Kenyans in general, their very love of white idiosyncracies, eccentricities and excesses. As he mercilessly jibed at them in Kiswahili, they loved it all.

At the same time, people like George Mukabi, John Mwale, and David Amunga, based in Western Province, were entertaining Kenyans in social halls, open air threatres and over the radio. In the Coast Province, musicians such as Daniel Katuga, Charo, Paul Mwachupa, Fundi Konde and Fadhili William Mdawida, among others, were doing the same. This is the era that produced the national classic, *Dereva Kombo* by Paul Mwachupa, and the international classic *Malaika* by Fadhili William, originally written and arranged by Charo. Copywright to reproduce the latter hit were awarded to world famous musicians, over the generations, such as Bonny M. (Carribean resident in Germany) Osibisa (Ghanaians resident in Britain), Miriam Makeba or *Mama Africa* (South Africa), Usha (India) and Harry Belafonte (U.S.A.) among others. All these groups and individuals have composed and sung their own versions of the song in Kiswahili as it was sang by the original composer. The linguistic atmosphere in Kenya's music environment was such that foreign musicians resident in the country such as the famous Congolese, Jean Bosco Mwenda and Massengo Eduard; and the Zambians Peter Tsotsi and Nashil Pichen all composed and sung in Kiswahili.

In the transition period (early 1960s) there emerged three of the most successful Kenyan musicians: Ochieng Kabasselleh, Juma Toto and Gabriel Omolo, all from Nyanza Province. They all sang in Kiswahili even though Juma Toto, who mostly sang for the Coast dominated group, the Hodi Boys Band, could sometimes sing in Dholuo, while Kabasselleh eventually completely switched to Dholuo. Gabriel Omolo remained true to Kiswahili to the very end of his musical career. To date, he is the only Kenyan musician who has handled the explosive gender question realistically and impartially in some of his more successful songs. He is also the only musician in the whole of East Africa to be awarded the highest medal, together with a handsome cash reward, by his recording company, Polygram, as appreciation for success in sales (tens of thousands of records) of one of his most controversial songs about the ever-rising standard of living in Kenya, where many are left behind to wallow in poverty.

With this pioneering group of musicians in the pop culture, ethnicity took a back seat. As has been severally observed, all these musicians composed and sang in Kiswahili.

After the first half of the 1960s, however, things changed. Talents flared like wildfire. Radios blared music in Dholuo, Gikuyu, Kikamba, Kimijikenda, Kidawida and other Kenyan languages. Compositions were generally mediocre, although excellent pieces were recorded by a few individuals and groups such as the man who has often been described as "the true poet", Joseph Kamaru, and the energetic Daniel Kamau, nicknamed "DK" with his group the Lulus Band. These two sang and still sing in Gikuyu. (Recently, though, Joseph Kamaru has also started singing in Kiswahili.) From Nyanza Province, Kolela Mazee with his Shirati Jazz and Daniel Misiani, among others, sang in Dholuo. Kakai Kilonzo, from Eastern Province, sang in Kikamba but sometimes released Kiswahili compositions.

Even Coast musicians, who had traditionally composed in Kiswahili started experimenting in their ethnic languages. The veteran Fadhili William, who had epitomised Kenyan success in music internationally, made an unsuccessful attempt at singing in Kidawida. Nahashon Gandani sang in Kimijikenda (Rabai). Coastal bands such as The Hodi Boys, Bahari Boys, Hongera Jazz, Safari Sound System, Vibrations, all recorded some songs in Kimijikenda. But of all compositions of the Coast musicians and music groups in languages other than Kiswahili, only seven songs have made a national mark. These are *Hinde* (by Vibrations Band in Kimijikenda), *Ni wasi* (by Abel Kifoto and Maroon Commandos Band in Kidawida), *Simba Yunanguruma, Kokota Mlamba, Pekeshe, Mangale* (all by Bahari Boys in Kimijikenda), and *Msenangu* by Pressmen Band (in Kimijikenda).

Thus with this new wave, Kenyans did not record the success that Tanzanians (singing in Kiswahili) were recording. As a matter of fact, household names of successful musicians in the country were not of local composers but those of people from neighbouring countries resident in Kenya. One was more likely than not to hear mention of favourite musicians such as John Ngereza, Professor Omar Shaaban, Professor Junior Abu Omar, Charles Ray Kasembe, Wilson Peter Kinyonga, George Peter Kinyonga, Issa Juma (all Tanzanians); Samba Mapangala, Baba Ilunga wa Ilunga, Kassongo wa Kanema, Lovi Longoma (all Congolese); and Sammy Kasule (Ugandan) rather than local musicians. Incidentally, all these "foreign" musicians sung either in Kiswahili (as in the case of Tanzanians) or mixed

Kiswahili with Lingala/Luganda (as in the case of Kasule and Congolese who, sometimes, sing in pure Kiswahili too).

The second wave pop musicians in Kenya have failed to gain the all-national popularity enjoyed by the first wave group. Neither have they measured up to the height reached by their predecessors. Ostensibly, the death knell has sounded for Kenya's indigenous pop culture.

The final stroke seemed to have struck when some of the best ethnic-language musicians got involved in party politicking. Apparently, they succeeded only in justifying the Kiswahili saying: *Nyama mbili hazitafuniki.* Some famous musicians even became born-again christians.

As fate would have it, the void created is very fast being filled with (Michael) *Jacksonmania.* The popularity of the age-old, internationally recognised Sal Davies, Kelly Brown, Feisal Brown (these are Mombasa born Waswahili) and Chokwe, as well as the national favourites, Ishmael Jingo, Slim Ali, Safari Sound System, the Mombasa Roots Band and the Them Mushrooms is testament to this westernisation of Kenyans' music tastes. Incidentally, the most successful song of the Mombasa Roots has been and still is *Disco Chakacha,* which is a collection of Swahili *Chakacha* folk songs rendered in the traditional Swahili rhythms but spiced with modern musical instruments. We notice something similar with Them Mushrooms' success, whose Kiswahili song *Jambo Bwana* has already been reproduced by the Germany-based group, Bonny M.

The most worrying outcome of it all, however, is the tendency of the after-independence generation, to have pure western tastes. To be precise, this group unabashedly prefers American and British beats to indigenous and borrowed African rhythms. But then again, this is an excellent reflection of the attitudes of neo-colonial Kenyans. It is a stark manifestation of their age-old infatuation with the foreign Western cultures; unfortunately at the expense of indigenous African cultures; so everything falls quite in place, really!

The language of the gospel and television

(i) Gospel

It was noted earlier that Christianity fostered Kiswahili in Kenya at a time when Islam was stunted. With independence, this wave acquired even better wings. Kiswahili is still the language of the Church today as it was during the colonial days. As a matter of fact, as Kiswahili is fast becoming everybody's language in Kenya, so has the Church felt more confident in using it, especially as more and more Kenyans are leaving their ethnic homelands and intermingling freely in urban as well as in the rural areas. In recent decades, the trend has been that, even though in upper class urban areas on one hand, English is used in Church while ethnic languages are used in exclusively single ethnic group rural settings, Kiswahili is used in all other contexts. Furthermore, the largest percentage of gospel songs composed in Kenya after independence are in Kiswahili and many of them have been sold to adherents in cassette and vinyl record form. Hence, we observe that the Church has been one of the major promoters of Kiswahili in Kenya.

(ii) Television

With the advent of television in the country, Kiswahili has again been blessed with the most effective medium among the urban middle class, a group whose attitude towards the language has been persistently negative. (Most Kenyans have the radio, among other media.) Fortunately K.B.C. T.V. has more local programmes in Kiswahili than in English.

Hence the resisting middle class has to contend with Kiswahili. Members of this class do not have to feel that their patience and entertainment is overly taxed by this order of events. Nonetheless, Kiswahili is, through some good programming by K.B.C., once again selling itself. This has been made possible through highly entertaining Kiswahili half-hour plays such as *Fedheha, Zingatia, Njia Panda, Vitimbi, Nyavu, Vioja Mahakamani, Vituko, Shida, Pambazuko, Wakati, Tushauriane*, the first local T.V. soap opera, and *Tausi* second and most highly valued soap opera so far. Almost all of these are comedies, although sometimes, one or two plots may be tragic. Most of the cast (in fact all), manipulate Kiswahili more comfortably, more mother-tongue-like than the most articulate actors in the English plays, even though, with an exception of a few in the Mombasa-taped plays, all the actors in most of the above programmes are not ethnic Kiswahili speakers but are drawn from various ethnic groups; including Indians. English speakers are very self-conscious, whereas, in the Kiswahili plays, one never notices that the actors have memorised their lines, as they speak so naturally.

Uganda

Avoidance-avoidance conflict

Uganda and Tanzania took different approaches to Kiswahili. Whereas Tanzania, as has been observed earlier on, adopted an approach-approach posture regarding the language, Kenya was locked up in the middle-of-the-road approach-avoidance conflict, while Uganda was to tread a lone path, namely: a non-compromistic avoidance-avoidance conflict stance, quite radically opposed to that of her neighbour to the south (Tanzania).

Uganda's history of total rejection of Kiswahili is long, persistent and consistent. Yet the reasons for

Ugandans' rejection of this language are not exactly the same as those advanced by Kenyan Luos. In fact they could be said to be quite the opposite. For, as was pointed out when discussing the *Luo factor* earlier on, the Luos of Uganda and the country's other (northern) Nilotes readily accepted Kiswahili. In this country, it is the Bantu-speaking southerners who rejected Kiswahili with passion.

The situation in Uganda that led to the rejection of Kiswahili by the Bantus is more complicated than that in Kenya. Kenya's problem could be directly traced to the colonialists and their "divide-and-rule" tactics. In Uganda, the colonialists arrived when various socio-politico-linguistic groups in the south had already moulded powerful feudal states that were wary of any "outside" influences. Every kingdom viewed itself as the centre of the universe and any and all other socio-politico-linguistic groups were just not as good.

Then there was Christianity, which they accepted. Kiswahili, which was the native language of coastal Kenyan/Tanzanian Muslims was not only viewed as a foreign language but also as a threat to entrenched Christian beliefs (Whiteley, 1969). Quite a number of Baganda in the Kingdom of Buganda rejected Kiswahili on the grounds that it had no native speakers in Uganda.

A third reason was purely linguistic. The Baganda felt that they had their kingdom, their Kabaka (King), their institutions and their language(Luganda.) It would be a contradiction of logic and culture to accept a foreign language to eclipse the King's language (Whiteley, 1969). Furthermore, if Kiswahili were to be spoken by *all* Ugandans, it would put everybody on the same plane. As the Baganda recognised the cultural underpinnings of any language, they realised too well that if Luganda and not Kiswahili were spread in all of Uganda, that would give them a lot of influence over the other Ugandans. They did not anticipate that the other Ugandans would see through this and accept Kiswahili just to spite and resist the coveted impact.

It will be noted that literature on why the other Kingdoms rejected Kiswahili is almost non-existent. This is because the British favoured Buganda over all other kingdoms and thus most focus was on the Baganda and Luganda. It will thus be assumed that these kingdoms rejected both Kiswahili and Luganda for similar reasons: the need to guard their cultures from perverse foreign influences, and also as a consequence of cultural pride.

The Baganda resistance

Whiteley (1969) gives us the following picture of resistance to Kiswahili by the people of Buganda:

(i) The governor of Uganda, Sir W.F. Gowers writes a memorandum some time in the year 1927. The title of that memo is: "The Development of Ki-Swahili as an Educational and Administrative Language in the Uganda Protectorate" (p.70).

The most important message is the governor's proposal that Kiswahili be the lingua-franca of Uganda. The Baganda are up in arms even though the proposal specifically exempts their Kingdom (Buganda) and also Busoga. Another suggestion by the governor was that Kiswahili be introduced as an extra subject in Buganda, as well as in Bunyoro, Toro and Ankole (Whiteley, 1969, p.70). This would, however, not mean that Luganda would consequently be struck off curriculum; far from it.

(ii) The Kabaka's rebuttal:

Response to the governor's "provocative" memo came from every quarter within the Buganda Kingdom. From the highest authority, Kabaka Daudi Chwa, came the following statement:

> I feel, however, that it is my duty to add here in conclusion, that it is quite unnecessary to adopt the Ki-Swahili language as the official native language in

Buganda, and I am entirely opposed to any arrangements which would in any way facilitate the ultimate adoption of this language as the official native language of the Baganda in place of, or at the expense of, their own language (cited in Whiteley, 1969, p.70).

(iii) Rebuttal from other quarters:

   (a) Ostensibly, the governor's nerve so incensed the missions that they decided to bypass him and send their appeal directly to the Secretary of State in England. Whiteley (1969) reports that the bishops of Uganda (he does not specify churches to which they belong) reacted by drawing parallels between Kiswahili and Luganda, showing the latter's strengths against the former's weaknesses. They then suggested that Luganda and not Kiswahili be Uganda's lingua-franca.

   (b) It is further reported in Whiteley (1969) that Mr. Kulubya suggested to the Joint Select Committee on Closer Union in East Africa (p.71) that English and not Kiswahili be taught as the second language in Uganda. As to the governor's proposal, Kulubya's opinion was, "I should say that in most cases, it (Kiswahili) is being forced instead of being introduced" (Whiteley, 1969, p.71).

Kulubya's unequivocal resistance to Kiswahili exemplifies that of all Baganda who attended the 1931 meeting of the Joint Parliamentary Commission. This is evidenced by Ladefoged et al (1971) who report that:

> The commission recorded that it would be desirable to encourage a gradual change from Swahili to English after hearing African witnesses (all of whom were Luganda speakers) who were unanimously in support of English instead of Swahili. The dislike of Swahili arose in part from the fears of Ugandans of implementation of 'closer union' between Kenya and Uganda (pp. 88-89).

The mood of this powerful socio-politico-linguistic group was, thus, so uninviting that Kiswahili's fate seemed to have been sealed in Uganda in the 1930s. Yet in spite of the Baganda wrath, Kiswahili spread, first among communities outside and within the kingdoms themselves. Mazrui (cited in Roscoe,1977), describes Kiswahili's penetration in this country, by the first half of the 1960s. "It enjoys... an important status within the army and police, the trade union movement, and the professional ranks of the Uganda sectors of the East African Services" (p.3).

The second half of the decade saw Kiswahili change for the better, as it took several observable strides ahead. First and foremost, the law-enforcement body had to resort to Kiswahili (Polome, 1967, p.6). Polome's evaluation of this major step is:

> "It proves that it (Kiswahili) is the only suitable language for inter-tribal communication in the very heart of the kingdom of the Kabaka, in spite of the considerable efforts made by the *baGanda* to make *luGanda* the national language of the country" (Polome, 1967, p.6).

The second step took the form of a decision made by Makerere University students (who then came from all over East Africa) to use Swahili as well as English for the purpose of communication; and, at one time, even organised a very active *Society for the Propagation of Swahili* (Polome, 1967, p.6). Polome further reports that "since 1963, the University College (Makerere) has offered a comprehensive programme in African studies, in which linguistic study is exclusively focussed on Swahili" (p.6). His evaluation of this happy turn of events was that "the future of Swahili and other aspects of cultural life looks brighter" (Polome, 1967, p.6).

This trend improved with each passing year such that by the late 1960s and early 1970s, research revealed that Kiswahili was being spoken by a far higher percentage of students ... as a second language (Ladefoged et al, 1971, p.25) than either Luganda or English, in that order. Ladefoged et al (1971) further report that:

> A slightly larger number of men speak Swahili than Luganda, even when the native speakers of Luganda

are included.... English is known by far fewer Ugandans than either of the other two languages. It is, of course, a language learned in school. For many people it is not much used in other circumstances, and tends to get forgotten .... It is apparent that knowledge of both Swahili and English is greater among the younger people (and therefore must have been increasing over the last 30 years). But the percentage of people who understand Luganda as a second language has slightly declined during the same period (p.25).

This tempo may have been temporarily slowed by the ousting of Obote from the presidency, first round, in 1971 and the (many years of) chaos that followed the event. With the coming in of President Museveni in 1986, however, the situation not only appears to be going back to course, but is in fact, set to move at an unprecedented faster pace.

Indians speak Kiswahili

The third factor that led to the faster growth of Kiswahili despite efforts at blocking it is, against the remotest expectation, the Indian element in Ugandan towns and this element's vital trade links. Baganda and any other people may not have liked Kiswahili, but they were forced to deal with the Indians who dominated local, and in quite a significant manner, international trade. Fortunately for Kiswahili, urban Indians could only speak in this language with their African customers. Evidence of this is found in Polome's report to the effect that:

> In urban communities, the use of Swahili as a trade language has also been reinforced from rather unexpected quarters with the increasing influence of the Indian community in trade life. The Indian shopkeepers, although they continue to speak exclusively modern Indic Languages, (e.g. Gujerati) at home, they resort to Swahili for commercial relations with their African patrons and have developed a special type of Swahili trade dialect called *Kiswahili cha Kihindi* (Polome, 1967, p.6).

The situation described above is true of Uganda as it is, similarly, true of Kenya and Tanzania. To be precise, there is *Kiswahili cha Kihindi* in Kenya and Tanzania as there is in Uganda, and Indians speak this version of the language all over East Africa.

Independence

Apparently, the attitude among the Baganda to Kiswahili wavered little with the attainment of independence, even though the Prime Minister and later President Milton Obote may have been knowledgeable in the language, being a northerner who had also been in Kenya for quite some time before going back home to lead the political campaign against the Protectorate Government. The enduring hostile attitude to the language is clearly reflected in the following statement by independent Uganda's Acting Attorney-General:

> ... official language - that need not delay us. The official language of the Government of Uganda shall be English. Now I hope that people will not spend a large expense of time on asking the Minister of Education when he is going to be teaching Swahili and Zulu: I do not know what other language! We are concerned here only with the Official Language, not with teaching another language altogether, which is altogether strange. [Interruption] Yes, if you teach Kiswahili, you might as well teach Gujerati. Swahili is no nearer to the language of the Hon. Member than Gujerati. I want to challege him on that. No nearer. He might as well learn what they speak in Paraguay as learn Swahili (cited in Whiteley, 1969, p.98).

Kiswahili becomes Uganda's national language

For the reader who followed the story of Uganda's impassioned struggle against Kiswahili earlier in this chapter, the heading above will strike home as amazing, and very strange indeed; but it is as true as there is truth! Against such a hostile background, making Kiswahili the national language of Uganda would be one of the most arbitrary decisions ever made in the whole history of the country, and it would require an arbitrary character to do so. That arbitrary character was found in the person of General Field Marshal Idi Amin, the third president of the Republic of Uganda.

During his eight years as the number one citizen of Uganda, ... what has been called eight years of misrule (from 1971 to1979), Idi Amin is well remembered for the many snap decisions he made. One of these decisions was to declare Kiswahili the all-Uganda national language. Why he made that decision was known only to himself. Most significant here is that subsequent presidents and their equivalents never reversed the decision. From President Lule, to President Binaisa, to Paul Muwanga (not president), to Obote (second time round) to Titus Okello, to the current president, Yoweri Museveni, everyone seemed to want the status quo maintained. And so officially, Uganda, recalcitrant though she was, had eventually to bow to the sheer force of circumstances and accept the common heritage in East and Central Africa: Kiswahili, the lingua franca.

Kiswahili-speaking presidents

Uganda has had four Kiswahili-speaking presidents so far. Obote, Idi Amin, Okello and Yoweri Museveni. This detail is of utmost importance since in most African countries, things seem to move only when the President is personally involved.

Of the four Kiswahili-speaking presidents, only two have used it officially or semi-officially. These are Idi Amin and Yoweri Museveni. The latter, for example, is reputed to have gone down in history by, as is claimed, addressing Dar-es-Salaam University students and staff in Kiswahili during the course of an official visit to the Republic of Tanzania (the University of Dar is the president's alma mater). This act must have sent a message to the Ugandans at large, listening to their president over the radio; that at home they may speak

Luganda, Rutooro, Runyoro, Runyankore, Rukiga, Lugbara, Ateso, Ngakarimjong etc, but elsewhere in East and Central Africa, they will benefit a lot with a knowledge of Kiswahili, especially whenever they want to communicate with various people of diverse classes. More significantly, the president's address may have served as a pointer to the direction of future language policy in Uganda, as subsequent events would prove. In fact the president addressed Kenyans mainly in Kiswahili when he and his Tanzanian counterpart attended the thirtieth anniversary of Kenya as a Republic. He did the same during President Moi's second multi-party swearing-in ceremony in January, 1998.

President Museveni speaks!

The ears of Kiswahili promoters and enthusiasts must have been tickled a great deal when President Museveni, mounted on a platform in Uganda, made direct reference to Kiswahili, for the first time since he became president. The president had, via Radio Uganda, underscored the urgent need to develop a regional lingua franca in East and Central Africa. According to a Mr. Kawooya, a lecturer in Methods of Teaching Kiswahili at Kenyatta University and one of the top Ugandan Kiswahili experts, the president had suggested that Kiswahili, and Lingala if need be, be developed for that purpose. Part of the text of Mr. Museveni's speech that addresses the language question is reproduced below:

> .... I would ... like to draw your attention to the importance of a common language that can easily be spoken by all the people in the Eastern African region in the exercise of integration. English, French and Portuguese which are currently being used for official communication are not good enough. First of all, the majority of the people can never speak these languages very well. I studied English for 17 years, and up to now, I cannot pronounce English words very well.... Secondly, even if the majority of our people were to speak these European languages well, that would not

serve the purpose of integration in East Africa - because language in each country would develop differently. This would perpetuate the present links between the individual African countries and the former colonial powers instead of forging stronger inter-African links in the region. These European languages are a perpetuation of colonial control and they are an impediment to integration. How do you integrate with someone with whom you cannot communicate?

.... Fortunately, we have a language like Kiswahili, which is spoken the way it is written. In Zaire, there is Lingala which I hear is easy to learn. So let us address ourselves to this question of language.... *I would therefore, like to recommend the use of Kiswahili in much of eastern and central Africa so as to solve this problem.* We should also examine the possibility of using other African languages like Lingala to further the cause of African integration (Museveni, 1990, pp.8-9).

If this is to be viewed as "the tip of the iceberg" - an indication of things ahead - as to future language policies in Uganda, then the tentative conclusion to be drawn here is that "there is a light at the end of the tunnel". We may thus take Professor Ali Mazrui's prediction which, at the time it was made, sounded like wishful thinking to the effect that "Swahili... is on its way to conquering all Ugandan towns and cities", seriously (cited in Roscoe, 1977, p.3). As a matter of fact, it seems to have been overtaken by events and may now be correctly judged to be out-of-date. The statement is, hence, modified by the current writer to read: Kiswahili has very little battle left in its bid to conquer the whole of Uganda. Evidence can be found in a research conducted as recently as the 1980s which has revealed that "in ... Uganda ... the lingua franca tends to be Ki-Swahili" (McCrum, et al, 1986, p. 319). Furthermore, the potential for the language's triumph in the region, and eventually the continent, is definitely given added weight by the president's word.

The exiles factor

It will be observed that President Museveni, a native of Ankole, a southern socio-politico-geographical area where the native language is Runyankore, speaks Kiswahili today. This is because he studied for his degree at Dar-es-Salaam University for three years. He went back again as a political exile from Idi Amin's atrocious rule. As a consequence, he acquired and perfected his acquisition of the regional lingua franca.

The same process describes how the Ugandan Kiswahili expert, Mr. Kawooya, acquired the language. Like his president, Kawooya was a degree student at the University of Dar-es-Salaam. After graduation, he went back to Uganda where he stayed until Amin's wrath fell on intellectuals and other people of that nation; it is then that he took a safe route to Kenya as did many others.

Another group of Southern Ugandan speakers of Kiswahili comprises thousands of ordinary people who took refuge in Tanzania and Kenya when Presidents Amin and Obote were wreaking havoc on their own country. As most of these people settled in the marginal areas of towns where Kiswahili was spoken all the time, (Kenya and Tanzania) they had to learn Kiswahili for their very survival. The exodus back to Uganda, now that things appear to be permanently settling back to normalcy, brings with it a fresh insurge of large numbers of Kiswahili speakers to the land where, as of legend, this language faced most articulate resistance.

The Democratic Republic of Congo

Congo is a large country with a current population of more than 24 million people who speak over 200 different languages (Whiteley, 1969). Of these, four major languages are spoken by large groups of people. These are Kiswahili, Tchiluba, Kikongo and Lingala (Whiteley, 1969). These languages are spoken cross-ethnically in different regions of the country. The status of Kiswahili in this melting pot of languages and socio-politico-linguistic groupings is that it appears to be, as yet, indeterminate as it has always been.

The rise of Kiswahili in Congo historically

Whiteley (1969) has outlined Kiswahili's development in Congo thus:

(i) Kiswahili seems to have the youngest history in this country compared to its penetration in the other countries in the rest of the region where it is spoken. It owes its introduction and initial spread to the caravans of the slave trader, Tippu Tip, the son of an Arab father and a Swahili mother, who lived between 1870 and 1884 (Whiteley,1969), the year of the notorious *Scramble for Africa.*

(ii) By 1884, a sizeable number of Waswahili had already settled in Congo and had established a native Kiswahili-speaking population around Lake Tanganyika and to the North and South. These settlers and the peoples they had incorporated into their group resisted Belgian colonisation (Whiteley, 1969). It would appear that they went to war protesting the setting up of the Congo Free State... but...were defeated by Belgians (Whiteley, 1969, p. 72). The language of these people came to be known as Kingwana from what they called themselves: *Bangwana*, meaning noblemen.

(iii) Another group of Kiswahili speakers settled in Shaba Province (then Katanga) and the Eastern areas. These spoke a dialect closer to East African standard Kiswahili as the first batch were soldiers and recruits from Zanzibar (Whiteley, 1969).

(iv) By the time Shaba became a mining industrial area, Kiswahili appears to have already become a well established language in most of the eastern area from the north to the south. The workers that streamed to the mines from these areas thus spoke Kiswahili of one form or another. This had the effect of producing in Katanga an urban population who (sic) used a form of Swahili as a mother tongue (Whiteley, 1969, p.72).

(v) Unlike in Uganda where most missions opposed Kiswahili, in Congo the missions used Kiswahili as the language of instruction in the lower forms of primary school (Whiteley, 1969, p.72). As in Uganda, the colonial administration used Kiswahili for administrative purposes.

(vi) As Kiswahili was expanding, it mixed with other Congolese languages and a clash was inevitable. The main rivals were Lingala, Luba, Kongo and Mongo (Whiteley, 1969, p.72).

Colonial administration language policy

The Belgians wanted a common tongue that all the country could use. They realised that French would not be that mass language but rather, it would end up being the language of a few privileged African elites. They therefore ruled it out and instead felt strongly that the most appropriate language must be an African tongue.

As the eye fell on Kiswahili, scrutiny revealed the language's glaring problems. There was the question of the dialects. Whiteley (1969) points out that the Kisangani dialect differed from the Katanga one and these two differed from that spoken around the shores of Lake Tanganyika (p.73). The greatest problem however was resistance from the Africans themselves. They raised various objections:

(i) Kiswahili was not a Congolese language.
(ii) It propagated Islam.
(iii) It was British East Africa's official language (Whiteley, 1969, p.73).

Much later, Kiswahili received strong support from some quarters in the colony. Points raised in support of the language included the following:

(i) It had been used in the country for many years.

(ii) It had a considerable literature and had already been standardised.

(iii) Its use in the Congo would immediately create a large Swahili-speaking block from the East to the West coast, as well as opening up the possibilities of links with the British-administered area of East Africa" (Whiteley, 1969, p.73).

Although these were strong points in favour of Kiswahili, it was not chosen, and neither was any African language. The foreign language, French, was chosen inspite of its potential to create a tiny minority class of "privileged" fluent African speakers on one hand, and a majority that could not speak it at all on the other.

Independence

By independence in 1960, Kiswahili was still confined to its large cluster of speakers in the eastern and southeastern parts of the country (Whiteley, 1969). There was also a certain amount of secular and religious reading material, several newspapers and a number of language courses (Whiteley, 1969, p.73) in Kiswahili.

A few years later, things seem to have changed somehow. Polome, (1967) reports that in the mining towns, people from different ethnic groups, and particularly children, resorted to Kiswahili for communication. He also informs us that in these towns there were a lot of cases of intermarriage among people who speak non-mutually intelligible languages (Polome 1967). When this happened, Polome says, the married couples resorted to Kiswahili and their offspring spoke Kiswahili as their mother tongue. This is also true in Kenya, Tanzania and all Kiswahili-speaking areas. Polome concludes that the prospects for Swahili in these urban communities are accordingly very bright (p.8). He concludes:

> Widespread as it is, Swahili may often be heard outside its area of expansion since many Africans have come in contact with it, e.g. the Rhodesians sometimes employed as migrant labour in the Katangese (Shaba) mines or the Congolese of various provinces who have stayed for a while in the east (Polome, 1967, p.8)

The statement above describes a situation reminiscent of one mentioned earlier with regard to Ugandan exiles in Kenya and Tanzania. Note that this is not an isolated situation of little significance. On the contrary, it will be noted that Swahilisation of people from African countries outside the Kiswahili-speaking region is, indeed, widespread. It is now common knowledge that thousands of Zimbabweans, evading former white Prime Minister Ian Smith's vengeance against them for waging a war of liberation, were settled in Southern Tanzania by the Tanzanian authorities, pending full liberation. These refugees and their Tanzanian-born children became proficient Kiswahili speakers. And even though a few opted to become full citizens of Tanzania after Zimbabwe's independence in 1980, the majority have either already gone back to their country or intend to go back in future. Together with the Zimbabweans from the Shaba mining area, those returnees make up a significant number of Kiswahili speakers in Zimbabwe.

Related to this is another open secret about hundreds of ANC cadres and their families in ANC military camps in Southern Tanzania (the ones "secretly" visited by Mr. Nelson Mandela in 1990). As with the Zimbabweans, this group would go back home with a present to their full-of-potential nation, viz: the most dynamic language in modern Africa: Kiswahili. And the most fortunate thing is that this awareness is not lacking in the future pluralistic nation. To wit, the president of South Africa, Mr. Mandela himself fluently said: *Habari yako Mwalimu Nyerere*, when they met for the first time in many years. He could have chosen to greet the former president of Tanzania in English, a language in which they are both known to be very proficient. His decision to greet his host in Kiswahili may be symbolic of the shape they may both want future regional or continental integration to take.

Language of pop

Congolese musicians have traditionally been known to sing mainly in Lingala. Mixing Lingala and Kiswahili in their songs is quite a common feature, nevertheless. Furthermore, some of the most famous Congolese singers such as Le Maestro, the late Lwambo Lwanzo Makiadi, Tabu Ley, Ilunga Ilunga, Mbilia Bel and Faya Tess, Moreno Batamba, Samba Mapangala among others, have recorded some of the most successful, purely Kiswahili pop songs to date.

Chapter Seven

Kiswahili in the Rest of Africa

Africa: The Tower of Babel

Africa's approach to the language question has always brought great confoundment to the people in question. Africans have often been baffled by their wealth in languages. This bafflement has been compounded by a nagging wish for unity, and urgently felt need to have a common, African medium of continental communication. Confoundment has occasioned every time the problem has been faced, particularly in the context of the obvious question of: which among the hundreds upon hundreds of languages is the best candidate to fit that precarious slot? The problem is best articulated by Roscoe (1977) who says:

> At one level the argument is simple and commands unanimity. African aspirations, ideally, should be expressed in African languages. How can national hopes, with their special nuances rising from traditional societies and their values inherited from a non-European ethic, resonate in people's hearts via a language which is firstly alien, the product of a foreign way of life and world view, and secondly spoken by only a small minority? (p.l).

On this face of the coin, the waters are crystal clear. On the other side of the same coin, however, the question becomes more complicated; and this other face is analysed by Roscoe (1977) as follows:

> The second stage of the problem, the choice of a solution, commands far less agreements. Each language has its spokesmen who know, feel, and can prove, the superior qualities of their particular vernacular, can point to its flexibility, its richness in proverb, its

simplicity for others, texts which have already honoured it, and the speed with which it is spreading among neighbouring groups. Newspaper columns in East, West and Central Africa have long carried rhetoric of language apostles; and the charms of small languages like Lugwe are as likely to be canvassed as those of major tongues like Hausa, Yoruba, or Chichewa. *But power now lies with central governments* (italics added), and given the sentitive nature of language issues, even in a world of increasing centralisation, only a foolish statesman would dare impose one language on a nation without the clear support of the majority.

Hence, the attractions of English, French, or Portuguese remain, either for politician, scholar, businessman, industrialist, or writer (p.2).

In the above situation, "*des langues d'importation europeenne*" would seem to have won the battle by default. However, developments in Africa have shown that winning a battle, any battle, cannot be easy. This is reflected in the struggle for status between the imported European languages and African languages, as the sudden and miraculous rise of indigenous national languages would testify. Of these budding all-national languages, Kiswahili is proving to be a potent force. This is evidenced by its varied supporters, some of them real strong voices in government as well as in scholarship, who have advocated that the language be adopted for at least regional communication purposes. This is underscored in Roscoe's (1977) statement that [In] "East [and Central Africa] there is a groundswell of support for the adoption of a regional alternative to English as a *lingua franca*: Swahili" (p.2).

The noted Nigerian writer and Africa's first ever Nobel Laureate (literature), Wole Soyinka, goes further than that, suggesting that Kiswahili be adopted for an even bigger role, to wit: that of a continental lingua franca. Soyinka's statement, first made in 1976, gains support in Ali Mazrui's advocacy for the adoption of five cultural pillars continentally. These are:

1. North African dishes
2. Central African(Congo) Music
3. West African attire
4. Southern African economic model, after apartheid has been completely dismantled, and
5. East African lingua franca (i.e. Kiswahili).

These five would constitute the core of true unity among Africa's peoples.

Why not Another African Language?

The writer of this book attended a gathering in which the newly honoured Literature Nobel Laureate would read his newest poetry to poetry lovers and his readers (fans). The gathering took place in one of the halls at the Columbus campus of the Ohio State University (in the U.S.A.). Some African greats, such as Ali Mazrui of Kenya and Cosmo Pieterse of South Africa were among the audience. It was a gathering of very serious scholars. The Africans in the audience came from all over Africa.

The poet gave a brief address to the audience to break the ice before reading his poetry. Of his poems, there was one about America and one in honour of Winnie Mandela's trials and tribulations, her determination and her eventual triumph (her husband was, as yet a year away from freedom). He alternated reading poetry and talking to his audience.

In the course of it all, one Kenyan student asked the poet about his stand on the language question in Africa. The latter shot back: "You mean about a possible continental language?" Then the poet said:

"I have said over and over again that Kiswahili is that language. It has all the necessary qualifications".

This was true enough, for the poet had gone down on record to underscore this very point while addressing The Union of Writers of the African Peoples on February

27th 1976, when he was the Secretary General of that organisation. He had, again, repeated his call (in 1977) in his address to the Second Black and African Cultural Festival (FESTAC) in Lagos, during which occasion he was presented with a Kiswahili translation of his play *The Trials of Brother Jero (Masaibu ya Ndugu Jero)*. The poet was thus well known to emphasise this point at every opportunity.

The Nigerians

Nevertheless, on this occasion, as perhaps on all previous occasions where the poet commented similarly, hell broke loose. The attack came from fellow Nigerians (it was obvious from their accents). They wanted to know what qualities Kiswahili had that were superior to those of other African languages. The poet took them on, pointing out that Kiswahili's history says a lot in its favour. That it proved beyond any doubt Africans' creative powers, for it was born out of Africans' own creativity and was a clear manifestation of such creativity. He also pointed out its ethnico-political neutrality and its spread in East and Central Africa despite obvious attempts to block it. The poet in fact, proved very knowledgeable on the subject.

The response came in the form of the assailants pointing out similar qualifications among a number of Nigerian languages. At this juncture, the poet categorically told an assailant that whatever qualities those (Nigerian) languages he was claiming had, did not qualify them for the O.A.U. post. He revealed to the audience that at the then current sitting of the O.A.U., delegates had endorsed the use of Kiswahili alongside the European languages used in Africa, and Arabic. That, now, Kiswahili was one of the languages of O.A.U! This was news to most of us in the audience. And it effectively brought the debate to an end... But not just yet!

Later on that week, a Nigerian colleague from Ohio University, Athens, one of the finest, most clear-minded African lady students revealed that the real reason behind the acrimony manifested by Soyinka's challengers on the subject of Kiswahili was that the language was the national language of Kenya; such a tiny country compared to Africa's "giant" (Nigeria). She further revealed that some Nigerians felt that Kenyans were unjustifiably proud and they were always competing with Nigerians. That seemed rather a challenge against Kiswahili again, this time round not from a trans-ethnic angle but a transnational one. At that moment, it dawned on me just how far we really were from continental integration.

The Zimbabwean

The current writer had a post-mortem of this debate with a Zimbabwean friend. The writer considered that, since the friend came from a newly independent socialist country, his ideas would go beyond petty ethnic squabbling and, instead, reflect a belief in the critical need for universal brotherhood; hence African unity expressed in a common African language. But the writer was wrong. And because he did not anticipate resistance, he was quite taken aback when the friend retorted:

> "Why not Shona? Shona is just as good .... just as qualified as the language of African unity".

When the writer had sufficiently recovered, he said to his friend: 'Shona does not qualify because those Nigerians who were bickering against the poet would not agree with you that it qualifies. Furthermore, you should have to start at home since, as they say, 'charity begins at home' .... You would have to convince the Matabele, who are fighting the Mashona long after the liberation war was concluded by both groups, that *Shona* is as good for them as it is good for the Mashona themselves in the capacity of Zimbabwe's national language. As it is, they cannot talk now as they are busy butchering each other. Then the debate rumbled on and on in that vein.

Soyinka's Word

What provoked all this hullabaloo was Soyinka's bombshell (he does not hesitate dropping them) on the 27th day of February 1976 when in a paper entitled "Yours in the African Cause", he lambasted African writers in particular and all the African elites generally for employing delaying tactics when it came to making decisions or implementing them once arrived at, regarding anything that is aimed at bringing a closer understanding among African people. The poet put the writers on the defensive by insinuating that instead of enhancing communication continent-wise (as "African writers", they had taken it upon themselves to do that), they were either blocking it or were not showing any willingness to be committed to that end. He challenged them to effect on and affect their decision to promote and enrich an African language to cater for the common needs of the populace at large:

> The Union finds it regrettable that twenty years have been wasted since the Second Congress of African Writers in Rome recommended the adoption of one language for the African peoples. Resolved to end this state of inertia, hesitancy and defeatism, we have, after much serious consideration, and in the conviction that all technical problems can and will be overcome, *unanimously* adopted Swahili as the logical language for this purpose. We exhort all writers to apply every strategy, individually and collectively on both national and continental levels to promote the use and enrichment of Swahili for the present and future needs of the continent (cited in Killam (ed), 1984, p.67).

The Organisation of African Unity

There is light at the end of the tunnel, nonetheless. For as has been pointed out, the Organisation of African Unity has already adopted Kiswahili; and the most recent session debated the setting up of an African Economic Community. ... And high time too!

With O.A.U.'s crucial decision on Kiswahili's status at that prestigeous all-African body, it is apparent that resistance to the language, even in West Africa where triumphant assertions about English's strength (Roscoe, 1977, p.2) were long recorded, will be tremendously weakened. This is bound to be so, more specifically since Africa is beginning to show signs of turning her eyes within herself; a welcome mode of confronting problems unique to the continent. In the light of this major decision by the continental body, predictions to the extent that the current campaign to endorse Kiswahili as a de jure regional lingua franca will eventually, probably very soon, engulf the whole continent will no longer strike anyone as yet another African grand illusion of the nature of Kwame Nkrumah's *United States of Africa*, but quite a feasible prognostication. In regard to the aforesaid, it cannot be long before Africans across the continent hail Soyinka and Mazrui as having had the insight as well as foresight to champion the right cause all along.

References

C.E.E.A.P.(1919). The Commission on *Education in the East African Protectorate*. Government Printers, Nairobi.

Gachathi, Peter (1976). *Kenya: Education Objectives and Policies*, Government Printer, Nairobi.

Ladefoged, P., Glick, Criper (1971). *Language in Uganda*, Oxford University Press (c), Nairobi.

Lumbasio, Petronilla Akweli (1990). *A Historical Study of Kiswahili in Kenya*, A Project submitted to Kenyatta University in Partial Fulfillment of Post Graduate Diploma in Education.

McCrum, R.; Cran, William, McNeil, Robert (1986). *The Story of English*, Elizabeth Sifton Books, Viking Penguin Inc., New York.

Museveni, Yoweri Kaguta (1990). Address by the President of the Republic of Uganda to the Third Congress of the Organization for Social Science Research in Eastern Africa (OSSREA) Kampala, Uganda (May).

Ominde, H. (1964). *Kenya Education Commission*, Government Printer, Nairobi.

Polome, Edgar (1967). *Swahili Handbook*, Centre for Applied Lingusitics, Washington D.C.

Roscoe, Adrain A. (1977). *Uhuru's Fire: African Literature East to South*, Cambridge University Press, London.

Sifuna, Daniel N. (1989). *Development of Educaion in Africa: The Kenyan Experience*, Initiatives Publishers, Nairobi.

Soyinka, Wole (1976). "Yours in the African Cause", in Killam G.D. (ed.) (1984). *The Writing of East and Central Africa*, Heinemann, Nairobi.

Wanjala, Ellam Khalagai (1985). *Probelms of Learning in a Second Language: A Consideration of the Problems that*

Kenyan Primary School Children Encounter When Learning in English with Special Reference to Mathematics. An unpublished Master's Thesis submitted to the University of London.

Whiteley, Wilfred H. (1969). *Swahili: The Rise of a National Language,* Methuen and Co., London.

Index

Abdallah, Abdilatif 8, 103
Abdallah, Salum 86, 87
Abdulaziz, Mohammed 5, 9
Achebe, Chinua 7, 26
Africa, Central 73, 79
Africa, Eastern 73, 79
Africa, West 62
African aspirations 127
African languages 77
African lingua francas 1
African National Congress 125
African Unity 129, 130, 131, 132, 133
African writers 132
African-American Jazz 106
Afro-Asiatic languages 26
Akida, Hamisi 8
Ali, Sheikh Mohammed 8
Ali, Slim 109
Alidina, Muhsin 8
American English 34
American media 34
American scholars 5
American universities 3, 4
Amharic 26
Amin, Idi 118, 121
Amunga, David 106
Angira, Jared 105
"Anglophile" Camp 41
Anglophone countries 58
Ankole 113, 121
Approach-avoidance conflict 87, 92, 95, 105
Arab-Descent Theory 25, 26
Arabia 74
Arabic 1, 11, 12, 14, 40, 42, 66, 79
Arabic influence 30
Arabic words 10, 40
Archives 6
Arthur, Rev. John 48, 75
Asian education 20
Ateso 119

Bacon, Francis 60
Baganda 112, 114
Bakari, Mohammed 5, 98
Baker, Mary 51
Baker, Samuel 51
Balisidya, Patrick 86
Bambara 1
Bantu cluster 25
Bantu languages 26
Bantu origins 26
Bantu structure 28, 43
Bantu words 36
Bantu-Kiswahili words 12
Bantu/non-Bantu divide 90
Batamba, Moreno 126
Beecher Commision 51
Bel, Mbilia 126
Belafonte, Harry 106
Belgians 77
Bergman, Father J. 76
Bhalo, Ahmad Nassir Juma 103
Bible 76
Bilingualism 79
Binaisa, President 118
Binns' Report 51
Bonny M. 106, 107, 109
Borrowing 10, 30, 33, 34
    in English 33
    in Kiswahili 35
    unlimited 42, 43, 45
British Broadcasting Corporation 7
British Council 73, 79
British universities 4
Brown, Feisal 109
Brown, Kelly 109
Buganda 113
Bukheit, Amana 103
Bukini 2
Bunyoro 113
Burundi 2, 76
Busaidis 80
Cambridge syllabus 20

Cameroon 62
Caribbean music 85
Chacha, Chacha Nyaigoti 5, 103
Channel Africa 7
Charo 106
Chichewa 128
Chimerah, Rocha 5
Chiriku 86
Chokwe 109
Christianity 47, 110, 112
Church 110
Church Missionary Society 19
Chwa, Kabaka Daudi 113
Cockney 62
Coinages 42, 43, 45
Colonial
 languages 19
 policies 89
 propagandists 90
Colonies 77
Colonists 76, 89
Commercial relations 116
Commission 52
Common language 76
Communication skills 57
Comorian Kiswahili 2, 3
Compulsory subjects 102
Congo 2, 3, 38, 74, 76, 77, 123
 colonial policy 124
 language policy 124
 spread of Kiswahili 122, 123, 124
Congolese
 languages 123
 music 85
 musicians 108, 126
Creative writing 75
Creole 53, 57, 65
Creoles 28
Cultural pillars 128
Curricula planing 68
Danish 28
Davies, Sal 109
Defoe, Daniel 33
Derek Nurse, 26
Dholuo 93, 104, 107, 108
Dictionaries 7
 bilingual 9
 compilation 8, 9, 10
 of medical science 9
 of technology 9
 vocabulary 10

Dutch 28
Education
 boards 19
 commissions 20, 21, 50, 51, 52, 57, 101, 102
 system 19, 20, 21
 vocational 50, 51
 western 47, 49, 50
Educational
 planners 68
 reforms 20, 21, 50, 51, 57
 reports 75
Educationists 100
Eliticism 54
Elyot, Sir Thomas 32, 44
English 1, 3, 9, 19, 20, 31, 73, 119
 borrowing 33
 concepts 11
 hybridisation 32
 influence 30, 31
 loans 40
 Medium Approach 51
English language
 as language of instruction 47
 borrowing 34, 35
 changing features 28
 development 83
 geographical spread 33
 germanic features 35
 hybridisation 33
 in Great Britain 60
 in India 58
 in Malaysia 63
 in Singapore 62
 question 57
 roots 33
 standardization 63
 status 31, 47, 51
Ethnic
 groups 90
 languages 110
Ethnic-language musicians 109
European languages 19
Examinable subjects 21, 100
Exiles factor 121, 125
Explorers 50
FESTAC 130
Folk songs 109
Foreign concepts 10, 11, 12
Foreign languages 56, 64

Freire, Paolo 54, 55, 65, 67
French 1, 3, 9, 10, 19, 35, 60, 64, 73, 119, 124
French Cultural Centre 73
Fulani 75
Gachathi Education Commission 52, 101
Gachathi, Peter 51, 101
Gachukia, Eddah 55, 56, 57
Gama, Vasco da 50
Ganda 96
Gandani, Nahashon 108
Gathwe, Tirus 105
German 9, 19, 20, 28, 35, 64, 73, 77, 80
Germanic languages 28
Germany 4
Ghana 4, 62
Gikuyu 14, 39, 94, 104, 107
Goethe Institute 73
Gorbachev, Mikhael 34
Government officials 50
Gowers, Sir W.F. 113
Great Britain
    colonial languages 60
    foreign languages 61
    national language 61
    official language 60
Greek 20, 34, 40
Gujerati 14, 19, 49, 79, 116
Gulag 58
Ha 91
Hausa 1, 26, 75, 128
Hebrew 26
Henry V, King 60, 61
Hindi 14, 49, 59, 79
Hussein, Ebrahim 84
Huxley, Elspeth 20
Hybrid
    language 29
    theory 30
Hybridisation 31, 32, 33
Hyslop, Graham 102
Idhaa ya Kiswahili 7
Ilunga, Ilunga 126
Imbuga, Francis 102
India 59, 74
    language policy 59
    languages of instruction 59
Indian traders 117
Indians 80, 116, 117

Indigenous African languages 19
Indigenous languages 56, 67
Indonesians 75
Inspectorate of English 55
Institute of Kiswahili Research 6, 7
Inter-ethnic lingua franca 1
Interpreted concepts 10, 11, 12
Iranians 75
Irish 62
Irish writers 62
Islam 75, 110
Italian 9
Jackson, Michael 87
Japan 4
Japanese 64
Jingo, Ishmael 109
Johnson, Frederick 9
Journals 44
"Jungu Kuu" Camp 36, 40
Kabaka, Daudi 106
Kabasselleh, Ochieng 107
Kahigi 103
Kalenjin 96
Kamaru, Joseph 107
Kamau, Daniel 107
Kamba 14, 74, 91
Kanema, Kassongo wa 108
Kareithi, P.M. 102
Karume, Abeid 81
Kasembe, Charles Ray 108
Kasule, Sammy 108
Kathiawar 74
Katuga, Daniel 106
Kawooya 119, 121
Kazimi, A.A. 19
Kazungu, Ezekiel Kadenge 5
Keats, John 62
Kenya 2, 20
    colonial impact 91
    colonial policies 77, 88
    Education Commissions 20, 31, 51, 52, 57, 100, 101, 102
    ethnic groups 90, 95
    language policies 86, 87, 88, 90, 94
    national language 94, 97
    party policies 90, 91
    writing in english 103
Kenya African Democratic Union 91, 96

Kenya African National Union 90, 91
Kenya Broadcasting Corporation 7, 13, 14, 110, 111
Kenya National Examinations Council 67, 68
Kenyan
  languages 67
  music 105
  writers 102, 105
Kenyatta University 5
Kenyatta, Jomo 94, 100
Kezilahabi, Euphrase 40, 84, 103
Khoi-san languages 27
Ki-Setla 92
Kibera, Leonard 103
Kidawida 107, 108
Kifoto, Abel 108
Kiimbila, Joseph 8
Kijiko, John 86
Kikamba 94, 107, 108
Kikongo 77, 121
Kikuyu 91
Kikuyu musicians 107
Kilaza, Juma 86
Kilonzo, Kakai 108
Kimijikenda 107, 108
Kingazija 3
Kingwana 122
Kinyamwezi words 36
Kinyonga, George Peter 86, 108
Kinyonga, Wilson Peter 86, 108
Kinzwani 3
Kipande, Ahmed 86
Kiswahili
  advancement 99
  Arabic words 10
  as examinable subject 3, 4
  as foreign language 3
  as lingua franca 22
  Bible 76
  borrowing 10, 35
  concepts 11
  Congolese dialects 124
  controversies 25, 26, 29, 30
  dictionaries 44
  experts 36
  geographical spread 22, 73, 79
  historical development 80
  Kenya education system 20
  Kihindi, cha 117
  language of instruction 48
  literature 6, 102, 103
  Luo factor 97
  music 85, 86
  new forms 13
  novel 104
  original words 10
  origins 25
  poetry 81, 103
  radio services 7
  rejection by Baganda 113, 114, 115
  rejection in Uganda 111, 112
  sanifu 36
  scholars 8, 9, 14
  spread in Africa 127
  spread in Congo 121, 122
  spread in Kenya 86
  spread in Tanzania 79
  spread in Uganda 115, 116
  status 31, 47, 50, 73
  status in Africa 73
  status in Kenya 98
  vocabulary count 10
  writers 103, 105
Kitsao, Jay 5, 87, 103
Kiunguja 3
Konde, Fundi 106
Kongo see Congo 123
Korea, South 4
Krapf, Dr. Ludwig 9, 19, 47, 51, 75
Kulubya 114
Kuria, Henry 38, 102
Language
  and culture 56, 58
  development 10, 11, 12, 77
  features 26, 28
  information, of 50
  instruction, of 64
  instruction, of 3
  of instruction 3, 21, 48, 49, 56, 59, 64, 66, 68, 69
  policies 52, 68, 78, 118
  structure 28
    origins 29
Latin 20, 32, 34, 40, 60
Latin American
  music 85
  Spanish 58
Lexicon 29

Ley, Tabu 126
Liberia 62
Lingala 77, 85, 119, 120, 121, 123, 126
Lingua franca 20, 76
   continental 128, 129, 133
   neutrality 1
   regional 128, 133
   rivalry 1
Linguists 103
Literature teachers 55
Livingstone, Dr. David 50
Liyongo, Fumo 104
Loan words 10, 30, 33, 34
Longoma, Lovi 108
Louisiana Creole 58
Luba 123
Luganda 2, 112, 114, 116, 119
Lugbara 119
Lugha Yetu Radio Group 13
Lugwe 128
Luhya 14
Lule, President 118
Lumbasio, Petronilla 98
Luo 14, 90, 93, 95, 97, 112
   musicians 106, 107
Maasai 74, 96
Mackay Education Commission 100, 102
Madagascar 2, 74
Maillu, David 65, 103
Makeba, Miriam 86, 106
Makerere University students 115
Makiadi, Lwambo Lwanzo 126
Malawi 2, 74
Malay 63, 75
Malaysia 63, 66
Mandela, Nelson 39, 125
Mandela, Winnie 129
Maneti, Hemedi 86
Mangua, Charles 103
Manuscripts 6
Mapangala, Samba 108, 126
Massamba, David 8
Massengo, Eduard 107
Mazee, Kolela 108
Mazrui, Al-Amin 16, 103
Mazrui, Ali A. 105, 114, 120, 128, 133
Mbaabu, Ireri 5, 88

Mbise, Ismael R. 83
Mboya, Tom 90
Metropolitan languages 73
Mganga, Yohana 8
Mhina, George 8
Migrant labour 125
Mijikenda 26, 74
Mijikenda languages 37
Ministry of Education 55, 67
Misiani 108
Mission stations 47
Missionaries 47, 50, 75
Missionary groups 19
Missions 123
Mkangi, George Katama 104
Mkelle, M. Burham 8
Mkude, Professor 9
Mkufya, W.E. 84
Mlama, Penina Muhando 85
Mohammed, Said Ahmed 84, 103
Moi, Daniel arap 100
Mongo 123
Mother tongue 2, 56, 57, 59, 65, 79, 104
   second 79
Mozambique 2, 74
Mugo, Micere 103
Muhaji, Muyaka wa 103
Mukabi, George 106
Mulcaster, Roger 61
Mulokozi 103
Mulwa, David 103, 105
Museveni, Yoweri 116, 118, 119
Mushi, S. 82
Music
   bands 86
   Congolese 108
   Kenyan 105, 106, 107, 109
   popular 85, 86, 105, 106, 107, 108, 109, 126
   Tanzanian 86, 108
Muslims 75
Muwanga, Paul 118
Mwachupa, Paul 106
Mwale, John 106
Mwangi, Meja 103
Mwaruka, Mbarak Mwinshehe 86, 87
Mwenda, Jean Bosco 107
Nabhany, Ahmad Sheikh 5, 9, 10, 11, 36, 42

Nassir, Ahmad 103
National culture 98
National language 3, 21, 65, 67, 78, 79, 94, 95, 98, 117
   development 97, 98
National unity 3
Nationalists 40
Navigators 50
Nehru, Prime Minister 59
New Primary Approach 50, 51
New, Charles 47
Newton, Sir Isaac 60
Ngakarimjong 119
Ngereza, John 108
Ngugi, Gerishon 102
Nigeria 62
Nigerian languages 130
Nigerians 130, 131
Njau, Rebecca 103
Njilima, Duncan 86
Njogu, Kimani 5
Njonjo, Charles M. 97
Nkurumah, Kwame 62, 133
Non-ethnic Swahili structures 38
Nyakusya 91
Nyerere, Julius K. 36, 81
Nyoike, Kimani wa 102
Obote, Milton 116, 117, 118, 121
Official language 3, 21, 65, 67, 79, 117
Ogot, Grace 102, 104
Ohly, Rajmund 8
Okare, Thomas 103
Okello, Titus 118
Oman 2, 74
Omar, Professor Junior Abu 108
Ominde Commission 57
Ominde Education Commission 21
Ominde, Professor Simeon 50, 51, 100
Omolo, Gabriel 107
Omolo, Leo Odero 102
Organisation of African Unity
   adoption of Kiswahili 132
   endorsement of Kiswahili 130
Osibisa 86, 106
Ouko, Robert 90
Pakistanis 75
Palangyo, Peter 83

Parliamentary debates 94
Pemba 2, 79, 80
Persian 29
Peter, George 108
Phelps-Stokes Commission 51
Pichen, Nashil 107
Pidgin 65
Pidgin English 62
Pidgin Kiswahili 65
Pidginisation 28, 33
Pidgins 28
   Kiswahili 92
Pieterse, Cosmo 129
Plays 111
Playwrights 103
Pokomo 26
Political parties 90
Politics 74, 76
Portuguese 19, 29, 53, 54, 55, 65, 73, 119
   colonies 53
Prator, professor 50
Prator-Hutasoit Report 21, 51
Protestant Missionary Societies 48
Punjabi 59
Queen's English 62
Racial segregation 48
Radio 86, 107, 110
   programmes 13
   stations 7
Radio station 7
Refugees 121, 125
Regional integration 119
Religion 47, 74, 75
Religious terms 39
Rendille 96
Robert, Shaaban 81, 84, 86
Ruheni, Mwangi 103
Ruhumbika, Gabriel 83
Rukiga 119
Runyankore 119, 121
Runyoro 119
Rutooro 119
Rwanda 2, 76
Sabaki family 26
Schools 93
   racial segregation 47, 48
Schools, missionary 47
Scots 62
Scottish writers 62

Second language 2, 79
Semitic theory 27, 28
Sengo, Tigiti 8
Shaaban, Professor Omar 108
Shakespeare 44
Sheng 14, 65
    vocabulary 14, 15, 16
Shona 131
Shungwaya 26
Sidi 74
Sierra Leone 62
Singapore 63
Singlish 63
Slave trade 122
Slaves 74, 80
Society for the Propagation of Swahili 115
Sokko, Hamza 84
Sokotra 2
Somali 26, 96
Somalia, southern 2
Sophistication 31
Southern African languages 27
Soyinka, Wole 44, 128, 129, 131, 132, 133
Spanish 58
Spread of Kiswahili 21, 22, 73, 79, 127
    political factors 76, 77
    religious factors 74, 75
    trade factors 73, 74
Standardisation 75
Steere, Bishop Edward 6, 9, 19, 75, 76
Stevens, Siaka 63
Students of Kiswahili 43
Subject of study 3, 5, 21, 43, 47, 101, 102
Sukuma 91
Sultan of Zanzibar 74
Swahili literature 55
Swahilised Arabs 2
Swedish Missions 76
Swift, Jonathan 62
Taasisi 6
Tanganyika African National Union 81
Tanzania 2, 74, 77
    bilingualism 79
    ethnic groups 91
    German administration 80

language policies 79, 80, 82
mother tongue 79
national language 79
official language 79
Tanzanian
    music 85
    writers 84
Tchiluba 77, 121
Technical words 39
Technological terms 29
Tejani, Jaafar 8
Television 110
Television programmes 14, 111
Temu, Canute W. 8
Tess, Faya 126
Thiong'o, Ngugi wa 19, 39, 102, 104
Tip, Tippu 122
Toro 113
Toto, Juma 107
Tower of Babel 57, 127
Trade 74
Translated concepts 10, 11
Tsotsi, Peter 107
Tumbo, Zubeida 8
Turkana 96
Turks 75
Tuskegee Institute 51
Uganda 2, 76, 77
    colonial policies 77
    ethnic groups 95
    exiles 125
    Indian factor 117
    kingdoms 111
    language policies 117, 118, 119
    lingua franca 120
    Missions 76
    national language 117
    official language 117
    rejection of Kiswahili 111
UNDF 56
UNESCO 19, 52, 56, 59, 65
UNICEF 56
Union of Writers of the African Peoples 129
United Mission to Central Africa 19, 75
United Missionary Conference 48
University of Dar-es-Salaam 6, 7, 36, 121
University of Nairobi 5, 6, 54

Urdu 19
USA
    multilingualism 57
Usha 106
Vernaculars 47, 49, 50, 51
Vocational education 52
Wahadimu 80
Wanamapinduzi Camp 40
Wandera, Billy 103
Wanjala, Chris 56, 57, 94
Wanyoike, E.N. 98
Wapemba 80
Waswahili 1, 2, 74, 80
    Kenyan 74
    Tanzanian 74
Watumbatu 80
Waunguja 80
Whiteley, Wilfred H. 19, 104
William, Fadhili 106, 108

Willis, Bishop 76
Wilson, P.M. 9
Wolof 1
Wonder, Stevie 86
Word creation 42
World Bank 56
World's languages 34
Writers 43, 84, 95, 102
Xhosa 27
Yahya 105
Yew, Lee Kuan 63
Yoruba 128
Zaire 2
Zambia 74
    Kiswahili speakers 22
Zanzibar 2, 79, 80
    language policies 80
Zimbabwe 131
Zimbabwean refugees 125
Zulu 27

www.ingramcontent.com/pod-product-compliance
Lightning Source LLC
Chambersburg PA
CBHW051527230426
43668CB00012B/1765